Backyard Grilling

Grill like A Professional !

Recipes for appetizers,
pizzas, grilled meats, rotisserie meats,
grilled seafood, BBQ sauces & rubs,
side dishes, salsas & relishes for grilled foods
and sweet extras.

Chef Richard W. McPeake
(Rib Stars™ BBQ)
&
Jim & Joan Cattey
(Smoke n' Fire ᔆᴹ)

D1114064

i

Printed in the United States of America.
ISBN 0-9718014-1-X

Visit RIB STARS™ BBQ at:
www.ribstarsbbq.com

Visit SMOKE N' FIRE^{SM} at:
www.smokenfire.com

TABLE OF CONTENTS

Forward (by Jim & Joan Cattey).................................viii

Acknowledgments.................................ix

Grill Basics (Gas vs Charcoal) 1-4

Fire & Fuel Basics.................................5-10

Tools of the Trade.................................11-15

Tips on Buying Meats.................................16-21

Food Safety 22-23

Spices & Herbs.................................24-28

Basics of a Dry Rub.................................29-30

Effects of Marinating.................................31-32

Specials Grilling Tips.................................33-38

Proper Searing & Grilling Methods.................................39-45

Rotisserie Dynamics 46-48

Cleaning & Care of Your Grill.................................49-54

RECIPES
Let's Get it Going Starters: 55
    Fajita Quesadillas.................................57
    Baba Ghanough w/Grilled Pita.................................58
    Grape & Brie Quesadillas.................................59
    Beef Satay.................................60
    Mini Crabcakes.................................61
    Cheese & Salsa Quesadillas.................................62
    BBQ Chicken Quesadillas.................................63
    Crab Stuffed Mushrooms.................................64
    Gorgonzola Stuffed Mushrooms.................................65
    Steamed Mussels.................................66

Let's Get it Going Starters: (con't)

Pesto Bruschetta with Red & Yellow Tomatoes...........67
Chicken Satay...68
Deviled Grilled Shrimp..69

Who Needs an Oven! Cracker Crust Pizzas:............71

BBQ Chicken...73
Pesto 74
Grilled Vidalia Onion & Pepperoni..............................75
Garlic & Three Cheese..76
Spiced Shrimp & Scallops...77
Margherita 78
Nostra..79
Chicken Pesto..80

Not Meant for the Refrigerator Grilled Salads:.......81

Grilled Caesar..83
Refreshing Char-grilled Chicken Salad.........................84
Grilled Shrimp Nicoise Salad.......................................85
Oranges w/ Grilled Fennel & Red Onion.....................86
Grilled Asparagus..87

Taste Bud Marinades: 89

Margarita Marinade for Chicken..................................91
Lamb Marinade...92
Tuscan Marinade...93
London Broil Marinade...94
All Purpose...95
Mustard Marinade for Shellfish...................................96
Orange Soy Hoisin..97
Fajita 98
Coconut Curry...99

Unconfused Infused Oils: 101

Sage, Garlic & Pepper 103

Rosemary & Pepper 104

Roasted Pepper 105

Sundried Tomato & Basil 106

New World of Grilled & Seared Meats: 107

Tuscan Grilled Steaks 109

Steak Au Pouvre 110

World's Best Burgers 111

Hawg's Breath Pork Ribs 112

Grilled Lamb Chops 113

Beef Fajitas 114

Blackened Filet Medallions 115

Spiced Roasted Whole Tenderloin 116

Kifta (Spiced Skewered Ground Meat) 117

London Broil 118

Seared Veal Scaloppini 119

Grill Roasted Orange Soy Pork Loin 120

Teriyaki Ribeye Steaks 121

Plump & Juicy Poultry: 123

Chicken Fajitas 125

Herb Grilled Double Breast of Chicken 126

Rub Me Tender Chicken 127

Scaloppini of Chicken 128

Margarita Chicken 129

Grill Roasted Chicken Thighs 130

Shish Taouk (Marinaded Chicken Skewers) 131

Brick Grilled Chicken 132

Simply Seafood: 133

Grilled Fish Tacos 135

Peppered Swordfish 136

Seared Ahi Tuna 137

Seafood: (con't)

Buttered Crumb Topped Scrod 138
Mustard Grilled Shrimp............................. 139
Coconut Curried Scallops 140
Proscuitto Wrapped Pesto Shrimp................. 141
Lemon Pepper Trout............................... 142
Grilled Lobster Tail Scampi Style................. 143
Cooking a Clambake.............................. 144
Spiced Shrimp & Scallop Kabobs................. 145
BBQ Grilled Salmon.............................. 146
Grilled Garlic Crablegs.......................... 147

Worth Raving about Rotisserie Meats:

Worth Raving about Rotisserie Meats:............ 149
Lemon Pepper Thyme Whole Chicken.............. 151
Holiday Turkey.................................. 152
Red Hens 153
Mustard & Herb Crusted Prime Rib.............. 154
BBQ Mopped Whole Turkey 155
Marinated Pork Loin 156
Crispy Rubbed Duck............................. 157
Minted Leg of Lamb............................. 158
Finger Sticky Chicken Legs...................... 159

Award Winning Barbecue Sauces & Dry Rubs:

Award Winning Barbecue Sauces & Dry Rubs:...... 161
Rib Stars™ Double "J" BBQ Sauce............... 163
Rib Stars™ Hawg's Breath BBQ Sauce............ 164
Teriyaki BBQ Sauce.............................. 165
Cajun BBQ Sauce 166
Backyard BBQ Mop for Basting.................. 167
Rub Me Tender BBQ Rub........................ 168
Rib Stars™ Hawg's Breath BBQ Rub 169
Memphis Style Dry Rub.......................... 170
Backyard Chicken BBQ Rub...................... 171
Rotisserie Prime Rib Seasoning.................. 172

Standout Side Dishes:... 173
    Balsamic Grilled Asparagus................................175
    Marinated Squash Ribbons................................176
    Grilled Veggie Kabobs......................................177
    Simple Baked Beans 178
    Marinated Mushroom Kabobs for Steaks....................179
    Slow Grill Roasted Garlic Bulbs 180
    Jambalaya.. 181

You'll Relish these Salsas & Relishes:........................ 182
    Mango & Mint Salsa..185
    Cucumber Salsa..186
    Gazpacho Salsa..187
    Melon Cilantro Salsa......................................188
    Papaya Pineapple Salsa....................................189
    Pineapple Salsa... 190
    Red & Yellow Tomato Relish................................ 191
    Warm Jalapeno Corn Relish................................192

Sweet Endings to the Story:................................. 193
    Grilled Pineapple...195
    Grilled Pound Cake with Fresh Raspberries............... 196
    Grilled Mixed Fruit with Almond Cream....................197
    Mock Grilled Bananas Foster..............................198
    Grilled Peaches with Sweetened Mascarpone...............199
    Grilled Pears with Creamed Gorgonzola.................... 200

Index... 201

FORWARD

Chef Richard McPeake's love of food was evident the first time we met him over 2 years ago. His Passion for BBQ has forged both a friendship and working collaboration that brings you to this incredible grilling resource.

Grilling is often one of the most misrepresented forms of cooking. Just get a fire and slap some food on it, right? Well, our forefathers certainly did that. But understanding the options and the possibilities now, that can take us somewhere. Once a few simple culinary principles become clear, a whole vista of new "non grill" foods start making sense out on your trusty ol' grill.

At a recent party that Richard hosted, we were presented with a broad range of culinary treats, from appetizers thru the main course to an awesome creme brulee´, all from his grill. The range of foods prepared would stagger some, however this is the beauty of what simply prepared and properly cooked foods will do for you, ... they will blow your socks off!

Richard's no-nonsense approach strips away the fluff, and leaves you with a clear and simple way to grill. Everyone knows that man has always cooked on fire, but the ability to master the flame (no matter the fuel) and understand the pathways, ahh... there's the rub, and Richard masterfully sheds light on that as well. So read on, enjoy and by the way you may want to pre warm that grill in advance, your gonna get hungry!

Jim & Joan Cattey
Smoke N' Fire

ACKNOWLEDGMENTS

I would like to thank my good friends at Smoke N' Fire, Jim & Joan Cattey. Their help and encouragement, in addition to the information on grills and knowledge they have learned over the years, was invaluable. Their expertise helped make this book unique. The truly love what they do, and it shows in the attention and help given to everyone who enters their store.

To my wife, you are my strength and believe in my ability. You are not only my wife, but my best friend and soul mate. She encourages me to better myself everyday. She has been the best thing in my life for the last 27 years!

To my two kids, Jessica and Jonathan, of who I am so proud. They have given me a lifetime of great memories.

To my friends who shared in enjoying the food and recipe development, that ultimately led to the final recipes in this book.

To Nabil and Peggy, who have become not only great friends, but have supported my cooking career and believe in me.

And to God for the loving family and friends He has given me, and the talents that He has blessed me with.

Chapter 1

Grill Basics
Gas vs Charcoal

There are two main types of grills available on the market today, charcoal and gas. With the hundreds of name brand grills available, finding the right grill should be approached with a thoughtful and patient attitude. This book has been researched and all recipes were developed using the high temperature Beef Eater Australian Gas Grill and the Weber Kettle Charcoal Grill. Not all gas grills will produce high temperature heat.

Gas Grills

Smoke N' Fire's concept is that a grill should be purchased evaluating the cooking system as a complete unit, not by the individual components of the grill. If a grill has 35,000 BTU's, with a 6 to 8 inch air space between the cook grate and the heat source and 800 square inches of cook space, it will be difficult if not impossible to reach the high temperatures needed to get a charcoal quality sear. At the same time if you have a 35,000 BTU grill with two inches of space between the heat source and the cooking surface and 300 square inches of cook space, slow cooking will be difficult. The relationship between the square inches of cooking space (not including the warming racks), the BTU rating and the distance between the heat source and the cook surface; will determine the temperature that can be reached and the overall performance of the grill. Find a grill that allows you to use a variety of cooking techniques: grilling, roasting, stir frying, slow cooking, deep frying, and baking. The vaporizing system is a very important feature. Most manufactures are discontinuing the use of lava rock, changing to a cast iron or stainless steel vaporizer plate that is designed to divert the excess fat drippings from the burners and burn it off, to help stop grease flare ups. The most effective vaporizers reach infrared temperatures and should be perforated to allow air to circulate freely in the grill body. Grills are available with anywhere from 1 to 6 burners. It is best if a grill has multiple controls, as it will more easily allow both direct and indirect cooking.

Gas grills are fueled by either propane or natural gas. Usually, natural gas grills are only available at stores specializing in premium barbecue grills. If you choose to purchase or are currently cooking with a natural gas grill, be sure to have a professional hookup an adequately sized gas line to the grill. Better grills can be converted to either fuel type.

Fuel type will not change the cooking methods found in this book. There are benefits to using either fuel. Propane allows grills to be mobile and if you forget to turn off the valve, gas loss is limited to one tank of propane. I recommend having a spare tank available. Natural gas eliminates the need to refill the tank and the annoying possibility of being out of gas, ten minutes before the party starts. Gas grills are available in carts, deck mount units, in ground or built in units for islands.

Gas grills purchased from specialty BBQ stores have a wider variety of accessories available: wok plates, wok burners, griddles, rotisserie kits, back burners, smoker boxes, and side burners.

Charcoal Grills
Charcoal grills come in many sizes, from small enough for two people to huge party sizes; and shapes, including round, square and rectangle box shapes. Charcoal grills can be portable, built into an island or completely built with bricks as a fixture in your backyard. Better units have bottom and top vents, to allow proper air flow, some also have side vents. The air flow on charcoal grills is controlled by adjusting the

vents, which helps burn the charcoal properly and control the heat. An improperly vented grill will smother the fire, and make it difficult to reach the temperatures you need and may cause harsh flavors in the food. (See Chapter 2 for Fire Basics)

I recommend that you purchase a charcoal grill that uses charcoal grates to hold the burning coals above the bottom vents. Some have charcoal grates that can be moved closer or further from the food grate, which allows you even better temperature control. It is a good idea to purchase charcoal dividers or holders for building indirect fires.

Several types of fuel are available for charcoal grills: natural lump charcoal (my preference), natural briquettes, traditional processed briquettes or straight wood.

What's the Difference?

Several years ago, the Discovery Channel approached Smoke N' Fire to conduct a contest between Charcoal and Gas grills. Their objective was to find out once and for all, which type of grill produced the most flavorful food. The contest was held at the Kansas State BBQ Championship in Lenexa, KS. Smoke N' Fire picked the grills, a Good One charcoal grill and an Australian Beef Eater grill. The Discovery staff picked Chef Paul Kirk a.k.a. Baron of Barbecue to cook and the contest judges: six people attending the Lenexa contest, one person from the Discovery staff, the Beef Eater importer and Jim Cattey from Smoke N' Fire. Chef Paul cooked sausage, steak, ribs and chicken. The meat selections were eaten fresh off the grill. Not one the judges consistently picked food off either of the grills. The Discovery staff and Jim said the contest was a draw, Chef Paul said the gas grill won. With the food quality comparing to a charcoal grill, combined with the ease of use, the Beef Eater grill was impressive. We know of no other grill at this time that could accomplish this level of cooking, the grills ability to reach 950 degrees surface temperature is the reason for the high quality searing that allows the food to retain the juices and flavor.

With a better understanding of charcoal and gas grills you can now make a fully informed decision not only on the purchase of your grill, but on the type of fuel, fires, and proper techniques for different methods of cooking.

Chapter 2
Fire & Fuel Basics

It is important to start your fire around 20 minutes before grilling time to obtain the proper cooking temperature for the best grilling results. It will also allow any starter fluid time to burn off avoiding any after taste.

Some of the tools available to help you start a charcoal fire quickly and efficiently include charcoal chimneys, lighter fluid, gelled alcohol, wood wedges, fire starter blocks, paraffin cubes and electric starters. I prefer the gelled alcohol starter, it works very well and does not produce the after taste like that of lighter fluid.

Proper Lighting of Fire

Use a charcoal chimney with gelled alcohol starter. You can replace the gel starter with the starter of your choice or crumpled newspaper. Place a layer of charcoal, one to two pieces deep across the fire grate in your grills fire box. I prefer to use 100% natural lump charcoal or mesquite charcoal because it does not have any unwanted fillers or additives. Fill the chimney half way with charcoal, put a ring or two of gel starter, top off the chimney with charcoal, and add another ring of gelled starter. Place the chimney on top of the charcoal already in the grill fire box. Ignite the gel. Let the charcoal burn until 3/4 of it is white hot, then remove the chimney (using thick leather gloves), dumping the hot coals into the grill fire box on top of the base layer of charcoal. Pour another chimney full of charcoal on top of the hot coals. Leave your grill open until 3/4 of this top layer of charcoal ignites and starts to turn white. You are now ready to grill. The charcoal can now be moved around to achieve different temperature and heat zones for proper grilling.

FYI
Homemade Version Charcoal Chimney : Using an empty #10 coffee can (large can), punch 5 to 6 holes along the side of the can just above the rim on the unopened bottom (using a large church key). Once you punch the holes in the side, remove the bottom lid with a can opener. Straighten out the prongs from the punched holes. These prongs will hold the crumpled newspaper.

Starting a Gas Grill
Starting your gas grill is easy. Just follow the manufacturer's instructions. Make sure the gas burner value is off, open the hood. Turn the valve on the propane tank to the open position. Turn on the burner valve, after approximately 3 to 4 seconds, push the igniter. If the igniter on your grill is not working, I recommend using long wooden matches or a spark igniter gun to ignite the gas. Light one burner at a time. If the grill does not light immediately, turn the gas off and let it sit for 5 minutes before trying to relight. Once lit, allow the grill to preheat for 10-15 minutes.

Direct vs Indirect Cooking
Before starting to grill, you need to determine whether you will cook with direct or indirect heat. Direct heat is used when searing and/or grilling smaller cuts that usually cook in less then 20 minutes; ie. steaks, chicken breast, burgers, hot dogs, vegetables, etc. When building a direct fire in a charcoal grill, I recommend the following two techniques. The different styles will allow you to achieve multiple cooking zones on your grilling surface, that allow you to move food to areas with the appropriate heat level needed. The zones are important in controlling your grills temperature to ensure properly cooked products.

Center Mounded Coal Fire

This allows for a high heat in the center of your grill with medium heat towards to outside edges of the coal, while producing enough heat for a low heat at edge of the grill for slow grilling

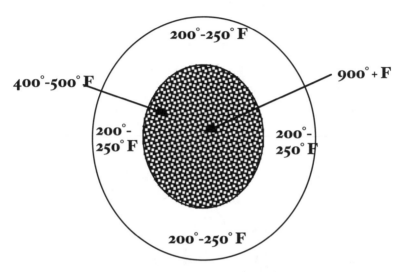

Banked Coal Fire (Left to Right Slope)

This allows for a high heat to one side of your grill with medium heat towards the middle of the grill, while producing a low heat at the edge of the grill for slow grilling.

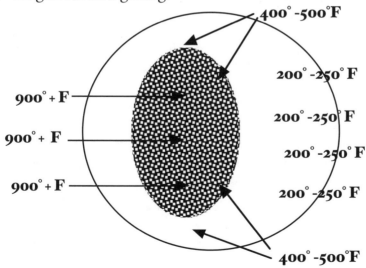

Fire & Fuel Basics

Make sure to use enough charcoal for the top of the mound to be about 3 to 5 inches from the food. The air flow on charcoal grills is controlled by adjusting the vents, this allows the charcoal to burn properly and control the heat. An improperly vented grill will smother the fire, and make it difficult to reach the temperatures you need and may cause harsh flavors in the food.

Indirect cooking uses lower temperatures with longer cooking times. Several different types of indirect cooking can be done by varying how the fire is built and controlled in a charcoal grill. The off set fire is built to one side and places the food to the other. This method is commonly used when using your grill as a smoker.

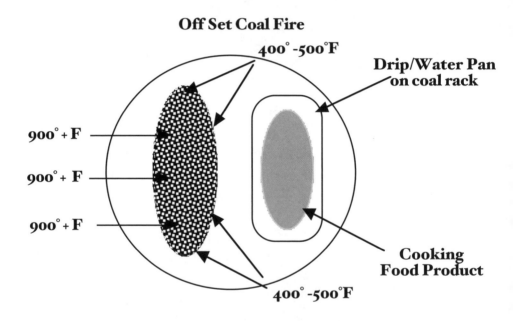

There is also the dual off set, with fire to each side of the grill and a water pan in the center. With the dual off set the food is placed directly in the center of the grill. Large items such as a whole chicken, beef tender, rib roast or whole turkey, cook well with a dual off set fire.

Dual Off Set Coal Fire

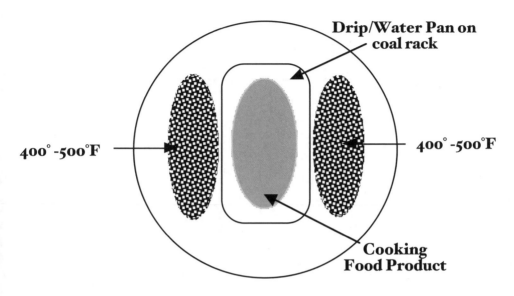

Drip/Water Pan on coal rack

400°-500°F

400°-500°F

Cooking Food Product

Indirect cooking on a gas grill, depending on the desired temperature, is achieved by turning one or two burners to low, on one side of the grill and putting the food on the opposite side.

Indirect Cooking on Gas

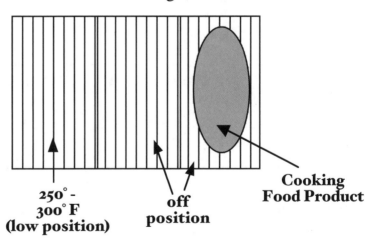

250°-300°F
(low position)

off position

Cooking Food Product

To cook with direct heat on a gas grill adjust the burners to varying settings to create multiple temperature zones on your grill surface.

Direct Cooking on Gas
(Creating Temperature Zones)

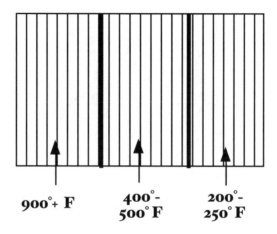

900°+ F   400°-500° F   200°-250° F

For gas and charcoal grills, use the hand rule for checking the heat of the fire. If you can hold your hand over the coals for only 2-4 seconds the fire is at searing or high heat. 5-7 seconds for medium and 8-10 seconds low heat.

Hand Temperature Chart

Time	Grilling Heat	Temperature
2-4 seconds	High	900°+ F
5-7 seconds	Medium	400-600° F
8-10 seconds	Low	200-250°

Using these guidelines along with the proper tools and accessories will allow you to properly control and regulate your BBQ equipment.

Chapter 3
Tools of the Trade

There are many different tools available for use when grilling outdoors. These tools are used in the same way for both charcoal and gas grills. Successful grilling starts with the proper tools. The basic tools for your grilling needs are described below.

Aprons & Hats
Every Backyard Griller has his or her own collection of aprons and hats. One for every kind of occasion or party is a must!

Baskets
Grill baskets are excellent for easier handling of delicate food pieces and are very necessary for grilling fish fillets or large quantities of small pieces of food. Baskets come in many different sizes and shapes. Make sure to get long handled baskets for safe handling and turning. These baskets work extremely well when you want to grill several different types of vegetables, allowing you to grill them together without turning each individual piece. Brush or spray oil on the wire grids before placing your food into them for grilling.

Brush
Find a grill brush that can get down between the grill grates for proper cleaning. The type with scrapers on the end serve a dual purpose for cleaning the grill and removing heavy build up. Fine bristle brushes,

with stiff 1/8" teeth work very well on grills that have wide spaced round grill rods. Stiffer thick teeth brushes work well for closer, thicker, flat grill rods or bars. Use only brass brushes on porcelain grill grates. One very important point that is almost always forgotten: clean your grill brush with every use, just like your grill. The easy way to clean your grill brush is with hot soapy water, rinse well and allow to dry.

Drip Pans

You may want to use drip pans when you are doing indirect cooking, not only for catching the excess fat drippings, but to hold water for moisture, since most indirect cooking will be a slower and longer cooking process. I also recommend using drip pans when doing rotisserie cooking since this style of cooking will also produce excessive fat drippings. Disposable aluminum pans are the best to use.

Forks

If you find the need for a fork, buy a sturdy long handle metal fork. Be careful when using a fork, since you do not want to pierce food the product and allow the moisture to bleed out. Forks should only be used to move items around the grill.

Gloves and Mitts, leather, silicone or fire retardant

Always have a sturdy set when grilling to protect your hands, to move hot grates or lift metal objects off the grill. Stay away from frayed cloth or terry cloth when dealing with open flame.

Griddles or Skillets, flat cast iron

Griddles are great for searing, stir frying and breakfast cooking.
Flat cast iron skillets function as a substitute for use as a flat griddle. They are usually available in rectangle griddles and come in many sizes.

Grids & Screens

Grill grids and screens are ideal for use in cooking hard to handle food, such as sliced vegetables, flaky seafood or small pieces of food. Most screens are made of heavy metal mesh. Some have a non-stick coat, but it is always a good idea to spray them with a cooking oil before placing the food on them. They come in many different sizes and shapes to fit most grills, and many have handles for easier use. Grill screens also come in the form of sauté pans and flat pans, making a very unique piece of equipment for outdoor cooking.

Mat
Pick a mat that is noncombustible to put underneath your grill. It will not only protect the deck from burning coals and hot ash, but help protect from any grease spills or drippings. Never place hot coals outside the grill! They can catch a deck or siding on fire. A breathable mat will keep the deck from mildew and stains.

Planks
Plank cooking is especially common in the Northwest part of the United States, but has become very popular everywhere in the BBQ world. These planks of wood add excellent flavor to your food, especially seafood. Most planks are made of cedar or alder wood. Some are thinner than others and can be used several times before discarding. The larger permanent serving planks are much thicker and are meant for both cooking and serving right on the plank itself. Most planks can be used on your grill, smoker or in ovens. The larger serving planks are not meant to be put directly over the heat source, however thinner planks are placed over the heat to burn a little, with the food directly on the plank, allowing the food to pick up additional wood flavor as it cooks. Make sure to follow the manufacturer's instruction for the plank before cooking, cleaning or oiling it.

Skewers
Skewers are used to make kabobs, whether seafood, vegetables or meat and come in two basic types. Bamboo (normally 6" and 12" sizes) and metal skewers (ranging in thickness and lengths). I prefer Bamboo skewers when doing vegetables and seafood, since they are thinner and these items tend to cook faster on the grill. It is a good

idea to soak the bamboo skewers in water for about an hour, to prevent them from burning before the food is done.

Metal skewers are used for large foods and longer cooking times i.e. beef, lamb, chicken, etc. Always be careful when turning and removing metal skewers, since they get very hot when grilling. When assembling skewers always allow a small gap between the product for proper cooking and be careful not to overload or push food too close together. Always twist the skewer as you are removing the food to allow any food stuck on the skewer to loosen itself and come off freely.

Smoker Box
Smoker boxes come in steel, cast iron and stainless steel. Buy one with a lid, it helps slow combustion. It is a great way to add flavor even when cooking with gas.

Spatulas
Spatulas are practical to use when grilling, just about anything, hamburgers, steaks, fish fillets, vegetables, etc. I prefer sturdy, long wooden handled, spatulas, since they are easy to use and don't get as hot as metal handled spatulas. High temperature rubber spatulas can withstand heat from 600° to 1000°. They will still melt if left close to the heat source, but do come in very handy for stirring beans and sauces, or for making scrambled eggs in a pot or griddle.

Spray Bottles
Spray bottles are great for two reasons; they come in handy when grilling over open flames, used to spray a light mist of water to reduce flare up and fires, and they can also be used for spraying foods with liquid flavors such as fruit juices or marinades. Look for spray bottles that have the filter attachment on the end of the suction tube, to help filter out spice and herb particles in the liquid so they don't block the spray head.

Thermometers

There are numerous styles and varieties of thermometers available, from small pocket meat thermometer to a digital remote thermometer. There are also digital probe thermometers for monitoring the internal temperature as the product cooks. These also come with built-in timers, clocks and alarms and in wireless versions. I recommend the digital probes for checking temperatures when grilling larger items, however, these probes cannot be used when cooking on a rotisserie, since they have a wire attached from the probe to the monitor.

Tongs

I like good sturdy restaurant quality tongs that bend at the back end and work by the pinching motion of the front end. Spring loaded tongs are great, but they will wear out over time. The real key here is to use a long high quality tong, to allow your hands plenty of distance from the heat source. I recommend a tong at least 12" long.

With high quality long lasting professional tools, you will quickly master grilling and searing techniques.

Chapter 4
Tips on Buying Meats

In this chapter, I concentrate on the meats most commonly used in backyard grilling! These are not all the food products available, but you will have an idea how to buy product, and which ones are the easiest to look for and use.

Chicken Breast *(Grilling)*
Fresh Chicken Breasts are the best to use, and most of the time use boneless, skinless chicken breast. The most common sizes are 4, 6 and 8 ounce pieces. Beware when buying frozen breast since most of these products are pumped with water.

Chicken Breast, bone-in *(Grill Roasting)*
These are great for low heat grill roasting. They range in size from 12 to 20 ounces. It is best to remove the kiel bone before grilling to reduce the amount of cooking time.

Chicken, whole (2-3 pound range) *(Grill Roasting & Rotisserie Cooking)*
Whole chickens lend themselves well to rotisserie cooking and slow grill roasting. Never use chickens over 3 pounds, as they are older birds and tend to be tough and dry. Tuck the wings under the bird before cooking to prevent them from burning. Air dry chickens, in the refrigerator uncovered for 24 hours prior to cooking. This opens the pores of the skin and more fat will be rendered during the cooking process, and produces a nice crisp skin.

Duck, whole *(Rotisserie Cooking)*

Whole ducks are great for the rotisserie. Most ducks are in the 5 to 6 pound range. They need to air dry for 24 hours, and cooked slowly to render the fat from under the skin. Fresh duck is hard to find, unless you know a hunter!

Fish Fillets *(Grilling)*

The most important thing about buying fresh fish is to know your seller. Many stores pass off previously frozen, thawed fish for fresh. Fresh Fillets should be bright in color and not smell of "fish". The smell is a sign of old fish. Also, check the edges of the fillet, dried out or discolored edges are another sign old fish. The flesh of the fish should have some spring to the touch. Salmon is one of the best fish fillets for grilling.

Fish Steaks *(Grilling)*

Again, it is important to know your seller. Swordfish and Tuna are the most common fish used for cutting steaks. When buying this types of fish, watch for a dark edge from the inside cut of the loin, this is the blood line and can be very bitter when cooked and eaten, have it removed. If you are preparing Seared Rare Tuna, be sure to buy sushi grade tuna. This is the best tuna for rare to medium rare grilling.

Fish Loins, whole *(Searing & Grill Roasting)*

Fish loins are usually sold in small loins, ranging from 3 to 5 pounds. They are great for grill roasting and searing. Look for tail loins, as they are smaller and easier to cook.

Lobster Tails *(Grilling)*

With several types of lobster tails available, it is important to know again, that tails are shipped frozen, so don't pay extra for thawed frozen tails sold as fresh. Most tails come from two specific groups, cold water and warm water. Cold water tails are the best. They are sweeter and whiter than warm water tails and cost almost double the price. In my opinion they are well worth the extra cost.

Pork Loins *(Grill Roasting)*
This product can be bought both bone-in and boneless. There are also many different pre marinated flavors available. There are two different ends to the pork loin, sirloin and rib end. The sirloin end of the loin is the single muscle end and is leaner. The rib end comes from the rib area and usually has two muscles and more fat. Personally, I prefer the sirloin end of the pork loin. Pork chops are cut from either end.

Pork Tenderloin *(Grilling)*
The Pork Tenderloin is primarily grilled, is very tender and needs to be treated like you would a beef tenderloin both in trimming and grilling. This product normally weighs about 1 1/2 to 2 pounds. They are also available in different flavored marinades. There is a big difference between Pork Loin and Pork Tenderloin, so again, know what you are paying for. Pork Loins are much cheaper than a true Pork Tenderloin.

Prime Rib *(Best for Grill Roasting or Rotisserie Cooking)*
This outstanding meat roast has lots of flavor. Most stores sell them in a half roast size, both bone in and boneless. I recommend starting with the boneless cut. Bone in makes for an impressive dish, but also takes longer to cook. You will want to use a boneless Prime Rib when using your rotisserie. A rotisserie Prime Rib cannot be beaten for flavor!

Ribs, Baby Back *(Covered Slow Grilling)*
Some will argue that these are the Cadillac of the rib family. Although I love Baby Back Ribs, I do like to switch between Baby Backs and Spareribs. I think that Spareribs tend to have more flavor. For the beginner, Baby Backs are the ribs to use. They are smaller (2 pounds and under per rack) and easier to cook, since they cook in less time and are usually more tender than Spareribs. Baby Backs should never

have any chime bone or flap meat on them. Baby Backs are also the most expensive pork ribs you can buy!

Ribs, Spare *(Covered Slow Grilling)*

Spareribs will weigh about 2 to 3 pounds. Always select the lighter weight ribs as they come from a smaller and usually younger animal, will be more tender, and have a faster cooking period. Spareribs have the chime bone and part of the brisket flap still intact, which is what makes the large end of the sparerib so thick. The flap is on the bone side of the sparerib, also located on the large end of the rib. Spareribs can also be bought fully trimmed with the membrane removed. Understand the product that you are purchasing, so you will know if you need to trim them.

Ribs, Spare, St. Louis Style *(Covered Slow Grilling)*

These Spareribs have been fully trimmed of the chime bone and the brisket flap, and have been evenly cut across the bottom so that the rib is the same width from end to end. St. Louis Style Ribs can be just as good as Baby Backs when cooked right. I use Spareribs and St. Louis Ribs interchangeably! They tend to be lighter in weight than spares, weighing about 1 3/4 - 2 pounds. Again, I prefer the smaller sized ribs.

Scallops *(Grilling & Searing)*

Several types of scallops are available. Buy fresh whenever you can, most frozen scallops are pumped with water and tend to shrink when cooked. Calico Scallops are very small Florida scallops and cook very quickly. (They also overcook easily!). Bay scallops are slightly larger. For grilling and searing, the best scallops to use are Sea Scallops of the 10/12 count.

Shrimp *(Grilling)*

Unless you live near the ocean or gulf, you will not find fresh shrimp. Shrimp is shipped frozen, 95% of the time, and most local stores sell thawed frozen shrimp in their fresh displays. It is best to buy the frozen shrimp and thaw it yourself under refrigeration, since the stores will charge you for the water loss. Shrimp is sold by the pound count, i.e. 16/20, 21/25, 31/43, etc. This count tells you how many shrimp are in a pound. I recommend for grilling using the larger size shrimp, 16/120 or 21/25 count, since smaller size shrimp will cook very fats and tend to get over cooked.

Tenderloin, whole *(Best for Grill Roasting)*

Outstanding choice, and does not take long to achieve the finished product. It's already tender, so cook just until you have a beautiful medium rare roast. Usually you will want a whole tenderloin for roasting. They range in weight from 5 to 6 pounds. Ask the butcher to cut the side chain off, trim the fat and silver skin (which lies underneath the fat). This cleaned tenderloin is referred to as a pismo (fully trimmed).

Turkey, whole *(Grill Roasting & Rotisserie Cooking)*

Whole turkeys are great for the rotisserie, and range from 10 to 20 pounds. Fresh turkeys are difficult to find during the off season.
Thaw a frozen bird completely under refrigeration. Once thawed, wash and air dry for 24 hours before cooking to produce a nice crisp skin.

Turkey Breast *(Grill Roasting or Rotisserie Cooking)*

A great alternative to a whole turkey, ranging in size from in size and weight from a single sided to a double sided breast. Turkey breast can be grill roasted very nicely. If cooking on the rotisserie. I suggest using boneless turkey breast.

Turkey Chops *(Grilling)*

Your butcher can cut them for you, however, you can easily cut them yourself. Just split the bone-in breast and cut the chops across the grain. They are great for grilling.

Remember that all meats are not created equal, find a reliable grocer , I prefer small specialty butcher shops, that maintain a staff of properly trained, experienced staff, that can help with high quality fresh cut meats.

Chapter 5
Food Safety

Food safety is the most important thing to know and practice for a safe backyard grilling experience. To protect yourself and friends from a food borne illness, practice these guidelines when cooking outdoors.

Buying
Buy fresh quality foods!

Thawing
Thaw frozen products under refrigeration or cold running water. Never thaw foods at room temperature. Foods may be defrosted in the microwave, as long as they are cooked immediately after thawing. Remember that the microwave is cooking the food.

Storage
Ensure proper food storage, store under refrigeration at 40°. Never allow food to sit out at room temperature for long periods of time.

Handling
Use proper handling procedures to avoid cross contamination. Wash and sanitize your cutting board between every use. Never cut several different raw products on the same board without cleaning it thoroughly. Wash your hands every time you handle a different product, especially raw products.

Equipment
Make sure your equipment is clean before every use. This includes, your grill, knives, serving utensils, cooking utensils and serving dishes.

Safe Internal Cooking Temperatures
Cook all food to the safe internal temperature for that product, to ensure that bacteria, present in all foods, is killed.
The following are the internal temperatures for proper doneness:

Whole Beef & Lamb: 145°
Pork: 155°
Seafood: 145°
Poultry: 165°
Ground Beef: 165°
Ground Poultry: 165°

Cooling Leftovers
Do not allow cooked foods to cool at room temperature. Cover food loosely and refrigerate immediately. Once completely cooled, cover tightly. Label and date the food.

Practicing food safety is not difficult, but is common sense.

Chapter 6
Spices & Herbs

This chapter touches on some of the more common spices and herbs used in cooking. This list is not the final word on spices, as there are many combinations you can try, and hundreds of different spices and herbs to test and learn about. This list is just a starting point!

Spices:

Allspice: Small berry, the size of a pea, dried to dark brown. Has an aroma similar to a mixture of cloves, cinnamon and nutmeg. Used whole in pickling and cooking meats and fish. Used ground in cakes, puddings and preserves.

Anise: Small dried ripe fruit of annual herb. Has flavor of licorice. Used in Chinese sauces.

Caper: Flower bud. Used in salad dressings and fish sauces.

Caraway Seed: Dried ripe fruit of an herb of the parsley family. Used in breads. Compliments itself well to pastrami style meats.

Cardamon: Dried miniature fruit of a tropical bush. Used to achieve certain Hawaiian or Polynesian flavors.

Cayenne: Small hot red peppers, ground fine. Used in meats, stews, sauces. Adds heat to rubs and seasonings.

Celery Seed: Dried seed like fruit of an herb of the parsley family. Has the flavor of celery. Used in meat and fish dishes, salads, salad dressings.

Chili Powder: Ground chili pepper pods and blended spices. Very hot flavor. Used in chili con carne and other Mexican dishes. Good for rubs.

Cinnamon: Thin inner bark of the cinnamon tree. Used in stick form and ground for fruits and preserves.

Clove: Dried flower buds of the clove tree grown in East Indies. Used whole in meats, pickling, fish.

Coriander: Dried ripe fruit of an herb which is a member of the parsley family. Used whole in pickles, poultry stuffing, green salads. Used ground in sausages or on fresh pork.

Cumin Seed: Small dried fruit of a plant belonging to the parsley family. Used whole in soups, cheese spreads, stuffed eggs, stews, and sausage. Used ground as an ingredient in curry and chili powder. Excellent in certain dry rubs.

Dill Seed: Small dark seed of dill plant, grown in India. Sharp taste resembling caraway seed. Used in pickles, sauces, salads, soups, stews.

Ginger: Root of a plant resembling the iris, grown in India. Root (cracked) used in chutney, pickles, preserves, dried fruit. Also available in ground.

Mace: Orange-red fleshy covering of a nutmeg kernel, grown on nutmeg trees in Indonesia. Used in fish sauces, pickling, preserving.

Nutmeg: Dried, hard, wrinkled seed or pit of nutmeg fruit, grown in Indonesia. Aromatic, slightly bitter flavor. Used whole, grated as needed. Used ground in sausage.

Paprika: Dried, ripe red pepper grown in middle Europe, United States and Chile. Pleasant odor, mild sweet flavor. Used to season shellfish and to color meats. Used in dry rubs.

Pepper (Peppercorn): Dried small round berry of tropical vine with small white flowers, extensively grown in India. Used whole in pickling, meats, stews. Used ground for general seasonings of meats, fish, poultry, vegetables and salads.

White Pepper: Mature berry with black coat removed (usually ground). White pepper is used in dishes that require a less pungent flavor than that given by black pepper.

Poppy Seed: Tiny, dark gray seeds of poppy plant, grown in the United States and Turkey. Used in some sweet and sour sauces and for infusing oils.

Sesame Seed: Small, flat, oily seed of a sesame plant. Used for infusing oils, marinating and as flavoring in Oriental cooking.

Mustard: Small, round seeds of an annual herb, bearing yellow flowers. Pungent flavor. Dry mustard used in meat, sauces, gravies, salad dressings. Used ground in dry rubs.

Turmeric: Ground dried aromatic root of turmeric plant, grown in the Orient. Slightly bitter flavor. Used ground in curry powder, meat and egg dishes.

Fresh Herbs:

Angelica: Green plant, grown in the United States. Leaves and stalks used in flavoring liqueurs. Used in combination with Juniper berries.

Basil: Dried small leaves of a herbaceous plant. Used in stews, soups, egg dishes.

Bay Leaf: Dried, aromatic small shiny leaves of laurel tree. Used in soups, chowders, stews, fish, tomatoes, pickles.

Dill: The fine leaves of the plant are used fresh or dried. The seeds are dried, must for making pickles. Lends itself well to mixing with softened butter for topping seafood dishes.

Fennel: Feathery leaves which must be used fresh, but the seeds can be dried and ground. Licorice flavored. Either leaves or seeds can enrich, soups, stuffing, sausages and root vegetables.

Lemon Balm: Soft feathery leaves. Resembles large mint leaves, nice lemon flavor. Adds an extra lemony flavor to herb butters for seafood dishes. Great with Scallops.

Marjoram: Dried leaves and flowering tops of an aromatic plant of the mint family. Used fresh in salads. Used dried in meat and poultry seasoning.

Mint: Leaves of spearmint plant, grown almost everywhere. Used fresh for beverages. Used dried in sauces.

Oregano: Dried leaves of a perennial herb of the mint family. Aromatic odor, slightly bitter flavor. Used dried in tomato sauces, pork, egg dishes. Used as an ingredient in chili powder.

Parsley: Two forms of fresh; curly leaf and flat leaf. Has a subtle pungent flavor that survives cooking. Good in stuffing and casseroles. Mainly used as a garnish of food. Adds color to spice blends.

Rosemary: An evergreen shrub. Pungent. Compliments, lamb, beef and pork. Used in marinades to infuse flavors.

Saffron: Dried stigma of a perennial plant closely resembling the crocus, grown chiefly in Spain, France and Italy. Very expensive. Used mainly for its yellow color.

Sage: Dried leaves of a perennial shrub of the mint family. Used dried in sausage, meat products, fowl and stuffing.

Savory: Dried leaves and flowering tops of an annual herb. Used fresh to flavor soups, salads, sauces and gravies. Used dried in stuffing, salad dressings and stews.

Tarragon: Dried leaves and flowering tops of an aromatic herb, native to Siberia. An ingredient used in vinegar to develop special flavor. Used in fish sauces.

Thyme: Dried leaves and flowering tops of an annual herb with purple flowers, cultivated extensively in central Europe. Used dried in soups, sauces, stuffing, cheese. Used ground in rubs.

High quality, fresh herbs and spices will allow you to enhance food flavors. Sacrificing quality for cost, is sacrificing flavor!

Chapter 7
Basics of a Dry Rub

THE "FOUR" FLAVOR STAGES OF A DRY RUB

All dry rubs are made up of what chefs call flavor stages. These four stages are:

Stage 1: Sweet/Salt - This stage is the beginning stage and should be a balance between the salts and sugars used. Usually, this stage is made up of equals parts. I only use Kosher Salt in my rubs, for it is a truer flavor and has no additives. I sometimes split the salt using equal parts of kosher and seasoning salt. For the sugars I use granulated, brown sugar or turbinado (natural raw sugar). Turbinado sugar can take a higher temperature before it burns, so it is a better sugar for dry rubs.

Stage 2: Color - This stage is just that, adding color to the rub to define the deepness of reds in your rubs. I use Paprika and Chili Powder for my color stage. (I personally do not use Chili Powder as my heat source, but I use it more for a coloring point).

Stage 3: Heat - Be careful in this stage, since this is where you can make your rubs too hot in heat degrees of flavor. I like to use Black Pepper, Cayenne Pepper & White Pepper. The tri-mix of peppers makes a good heat flavor combination.

Stage 4: Flavorings - In this stage you can add a lot of your own personal taste. I recommend starting out with Garlic & Onion Powder

Basics of a Dry Rub

(not salts) because they add true flavor. I also put Lemon Pepper in my flavoring stage (more lemony than pepper). From there it is a matter of personal taste! I like cumin, poultry seasoning, ground oregano, ground thyme, etc. Use your sense of smell and taste to your liking.

When testing your rubs, always remember to change only one ingredient at a time, so that you know what item changed the flavor! The standard rule to follow in making a rub is: 4 parts Stage 1, 2 parts Stage 2, 1 part Stage 3 and 1 part Stage 4!

Have fun with your rubs and enjoy yourself!

Chapter 8
Effects of Marinating

Marinating achieves several different effects and can be done for flavor, tenderizing and/or to add moisture. The effect you want will determine which marinade you choose for a particular food item.

Flavor
Marinating for flavor is done in short periods of time from two minutes to four hours. Food products can be dipped in a marinade just before grilling, giving added flavor to the outside of the product while it is grilling. This method also includes using the marinade to baste food while it is grilling.

Tenderizing
Long periods of marinating are needed to tenderize tougher meat products. This period is normally from 12 to 24 hours. An acid form of marinade will help break down the product membrane, making the product more tender. The acid can be in the form of vinegar, citrus juice, wine, etc.

Note: Marinating chicken breast and seafood in acid for long periods will actually cause the product (protein) to cook, and become tough or rubbery. For this reason, do not marinate these products for more than 4-6 hours.

Vacuum Marinating for added Moisture

Using a marinade under vacuum, will not only help the product absorb the flavor of the marinade, but it will also absorb additional moisture. This can be done by applying vacuum pressure to the marinating process by using a food sealing machine, a Vacuvin instant marinater or a meat tumbler (restaurant equipment) A vacuum method also allows marinating for shorter periods of time.

Experimenting with different full bodied wines and fresh herbs, will enhance your marinating flavors.

Chapter 9
Special Grilling Tips

In this chapter you will find some personal tips on grilling foods, and keys that will help you to be successful in your backyard grilling adventure. I learned these things over the past 25 years while grilling, everything from steaks to fresh seafood as a professional chef.

Baking

Baking can be a lot of fun outdoors. You can bake in a gas or charcoal grill very easily. Remember, you want your grill to act as an oven, use an indirect fire, at high heat. Place your baking items to the side with no heat, and keep your temperature between 350° and 400°. Use the same baking times you would use for an indoor oven.

Grilling with Herbs & Vines

Be sure that herb branches and vines are dried well before using. I recommend soaking and draining herb branches and vines before adding them to your fire. They are a great addition to flavor your grilled food, add them at the very last second before grilling. Learn to match your herb branches with each product. Thin herb branches and vines add an additional flavor when using them to skewer food before grilling.

Here are some guidelines to follow when combining herb branches with different foods:

Basil - Chicken & beef products.

Bay Leaf - Use lightly with seafood.

Grapevines - Outstanding for seafood!

Lemon Balm - Seafood.

Oregano - Pork, poultry and sausages.

Rosemary - Great with pork products and swordfish.

Sage - Chicken & pork products.

Thyme - Beef, pork, poultry and goes well with light flavored seafood. (shrimp, scallops, etc.)

Infused Oils

Infused oil is excellent for flavoring seafood and steaks. To make an oil infusion, combine olive oil with assorted flavor combinations. Fresh herbs and onions are excellent (shallots, garlic, red onion, scallions, etc.). Heat olive oil over a low flame until slightly warm, add the flavors, and allow the oil to sit at room temperature for one hour before grilling. Infused oils need to be made and used right away. Any unused oils need to be stored under refrigeration and used within a week. Never store infused oils at room temperature, since this can cause botulism.

Poultry

Start by washing poultry in a lemon water solution. This removes any off flavors that poultry may get from sitting in packaging. I recommend marinating chicken cuts, but don't over marinate since this can cause the breast to become tough from the acid cooking the protein in the meat. If marinating, drain the product well before grilling. Oil the grates and place the product on the grill. When cooking breasts and thighs, after turning the pieces over, I like to turn the heat down. This lets the product cook properly and stay moist. Poultry dries out very quickly.

Reducing Flare Ups

Flare ups are caused by excessive fat dripping into the live coals or onto the gas burners. Flare ups can easily be handled by using a spray bottle of water, set on light mist. Mist the area of the flare ups after moving the food product. Too many flare ups mean that your fire could be too hot. Move your product and give the fire some time to cool down. Always move the product during a flare up, since flare ups can and will cause off flavors on your food. Flare ups can also be caused by too much food particle and grease build up on or in your grill. Maintaining a clean and well cared for grill does a great deal helping to control flare ups.

Seafood

Always remember fresh here! Keep the seafood chilled until ready to cook. Wipe the grates of the grill with flavored oil before placing the fish on the grill. When cooking fish fillets or fish steaks, dip the piece of fish into a shallow pan of oil, then drain off the excess. This is a good time to use infused oils (flavored). I recommend using medium heat when cooking seafood fillets or steaks - enough heat to sear slightly, but not burn, as seafood is an easy item to over cook. I like using a fork and spatula to turn seafood. I use the fork to lift from underneath the fish and the spatula to turn it over, then use the fork again to rest the fish on as it flips over so it will not break up. Never pierce the fish with the fork. When cooking fillets, I like to cook them with the skin on. Start with the flesh side down and finish cooking on the skin side. This achieves two things. First, if you are new to cooking fish, the skin will help keep the fillet from breaking when turning it over. Second, if you happen to cook the second side too long, the skin will protect the meat of the fillet from burning. Once is cooked, the skin is easily removed from the fillet, this is also another way to know that the fillet is fully cooked.

Shellfish

This includes shrimp, scallops and lobster. These products are harder to find fresh unless you live on the coast. If buying frozen for grilling, buy IQF (Individually Quick Frozen). Thaw slowly in your refrigerator or under slow running water. Drain well. When grilling shrimp and scallops, I like to place them on a skewer for easier grilling and turning. Non-stick grilling screens and pans also work well with these items. Scallops and shrimp, grill very fast so just season or marinate (not more

Special Grilling Tips

than 2 hours) and grill immediately. Infused oils work excellent for these items, either on the grill grates or in the marinade.

Before grilling lobster tails, remove the tail meat from the shell and cut across the tail meat (bottom side) with small cuts, not very deep. This will keep the tail meat from curling up on the grill, while they are cooking.

Smoking

Grilling over a live fire in itself adds flavor to the foods being grilled and will produce some smoke flavor to the food. Additional smoke flavor can be added by using wood along with the charcoal. The wood you chose and how much wood you use will determine the amount of flavor added. There are many woods to chose from ranging from hickory (the king of woods, with the most powerful smoke flavor) to sassafras (which I love for briskets).

When using your grill as a smoker, always remember to use an indirect fire. Smoke cooking is a low heat, slow cooking process. If the grill hood has a thermometer in it, hold the smoking temperature between 220 and 250°, depending on what length of time you are smoking. If the grill hood doesn't have a thermometer you will need to buy an oven thermometer. If smoking on a gas grill, a small vented metal wood chip box can be used which sits directly over the burner or vaporizer bar, depending on your grill, allowing the chips to smolder, and produce smoke. Soak the chips in water, wine, or juice for about 45 minutes, drain well before using. When using a charcoal grill to smoke, chips, chunks or split logs of wood can be placed directly on the live coals. The size of wood to use depends on the size of your grill. When the meat reaches 120 degrees internal temperature, or after about two hours of cooking you will not need to use any more wood. Just finish cooking, using the fire of your grill while maintaining temperature of 225°.

Many species of wood are available in chips, chunks and split logs. If using split logs, I recommend using pieces no bigger than 12" long and 3" in diameter; or wood chunks, that are the same diameter, but cut into 3" to 4" pieces. Remember only a small amount (enough chips to fill the smoker box, 3 to 4 chunks, 2 split logs) of wood is needed when you are grilling on a charcoal grill. Add the wood just before you start to grill, so that it begins to smoke as you begin to cook.

Jim's' Smoke n' Fire Wood Smoke and Meat Combinations:

Wood Species	Beef	Lamb	Pork	Poultry	Seafood
Alder	X	X	X	X	X
Apple	X	X	X	X	X
Cherry	X	X	X	X	
Grape	X	X	X	X	X
Hedge			X	X	X
Hickory		X	X	X	X
Maple			X	X	X
Mesquite	X	X	X		X
Mulberry	X	X	X	X	X
Oak	X	X	X	X	X
Orange			X	X	X
Peach			X	X	X
Pecan	X	X	X	X	
Persimmon	X	X	X	X	
Sassafras	X	X	X	X	
Walnut	X	X	X		

Steaks

First, buy nicely marbled steaks. They will have the most flavor. "Prime" should be your first choice, and "choice" meat your second. Allow the steaks to sit at room temperature for about one hour. This will help "bloom" (air) the meat and relax the muscle fibers. Season your steaks just before putting them on the grill. Seasoning ahead of time can and will draw the juices out, giving you a drier product. Use a flavored oil on the grates before grilling your steak. Once the steak is grilling, turn it over only once. Tongs are the best utensil for turning, never use a fork, piercing the meat will allow the juices to bleed out. Sear first, then slow grill to the desired doneness, for an extra juicy steak. Searing the outside will lock in the juices. Make sure that you always cook steaks over a hot fire, moving the more done steaks to a cooler part of the grill to finish. Remember, the key to a great juicy steak is to lock in the juice and flavors.

These special cooking tips will help you broaden your flavor selections and grilling techniques for your backyard grilling experience.

Chapter 10

Proper Searing & Grilling Methods

Grilling, whether indoors or outdoors, usually refers to cooking food products on a metal grill grate. Searing refers to sealing the surface of food on high heat, caramelizing juices and seasonings on the outside of the product. This is done to lock in moisture and enhance the natural flavor of food. High temperature heat and the control of high temperature heat, is the most important part of proper grilling and searing, when adding and retaining flavors in grilled foods!

Proper Searing

Searing is best achieved using a flat griddle , I prefer cast iron. Some gas grills come with interchangeable grates, allowing you to replace the grill grate with a flat griddle. If you don't have a grill with this option, use a flat griddle or cast iron skillet on top of the grill grate. Searing on this flat surface, seals 100% of the foods surface, producing a very flavorful crust on the outside of your product, while keeping the juices inside. A grill grate will work for searing, if you have a very intense, hot, close fire.

Searing in this method requires a form of fat be applied to the griddle before cooking. It can be butter, olive oil , grape seed oil or one of my favorites, infused oil. Be aware that when using butter it has a tendency to burn very quickly and cause an off flavor. I recommend most searing be done with grapeseed or olive oil.

Allow the product to sit at room temperature while the flat griddle is heating up. Use high heat, once the griddle is hot, apply a light layer of oil using a disposable cloth or towel. Spread the oil over the whole cooking surface. Remember just enough oil to coat the surface, do not let it pool or puddle, as searing needs very little oil. Too much oil can and will cause the product to actually boil and not sear.

Once the griddle is hot, season your product and place it onto the hot griddle top. Sear until the outer crust is formed, then turn over and sear the other side. After searing, the product can be moved from the griddle to the grill grate to finish cooking until the desired doneness is achieved. Remember, searing is a flavor enhancing cooking method and should not be used as the full cooking process.

Proper Grilling

Proper grilling requires attention to all steps in the process. Proper food handling is vital to make sure that the inner moisture is retained, since moisture loss will lead to a dry product. Proper heat control is also very important when grilling. Longer grilling items require a smaller less intense fire, whereas a quick grilling item needs more intense heat to give the outside a chance to crisp and sear properly.

Clean your grill well, removing old food particles. This should be done before grilling (after your grill is hot) and after you are finished grilling. Once the grill grate is clean and hot, , oil the grates lightly with grape seed or olive oil before placing any food products on the them. You can use a folded cloth or paper towel for oiling the grates.

After searing move your product to the grill, and continue cooking to the desired doneness. Turn your food over, only once! Turning too often will cause loss of moisture.

I have included this quick and easy reference list of various foods, with cooking times and temperatures.

Grilling Chart

Product	Method & Fire*	Cooking Time**
Beef Burgers (3/4 " thick)	*Grilling:* Medium heat. with direct fire	5 minutes on first side. 6 minutes 2nd side. (Medium)
Beef Kabobs (1 1/4" Cubes)	*Grilling:* Medium heat with direct fire.	2 minutes per side turning 4 times to achieve med. rare.
Chicken Breast (6 oz. boneless) (skinless)	*Grilling:* Medium heat, direct fire.	Grill for 3-4 min. per side or until done. (Internal Temp. 165° F)
Chicken Breast (bone-in 8 oz.)	*Grilling:* Medium heat, direct fire.	Grill skin side first. Cook 4-5 minutes. Turn grill another 6 minutes. (Internal Temp. 165° F)
Chicken Thighs (bone - in)	*Grilling:* Medium heat, direct fire first, then indirect for finishing.	Grill direct for 3 min. each side Indirect cook Cook until done. (Internal Temp. 165° F)
Chicken, Scaloppini (boneless & pounded) (skinless)	*Grilling:* High heat, direct fire.	Grill on both sides for 3 minutes. 4 oz. Flattened, 1/4"
Crab legs (split)	*Grilling:* Medium heat, direct fire.	Split legs in half. Place cut side of leg down first (meat half). Grill for 5 minutes. Turn over and finishing grilling until hot. (5 minutes)

Searing & Grilling Methods

Product	Method & Fire*	Cooking Time**
Filet Medallions (1/2" thick)	*Searing & Grilling:* High heat for searing. Medium heat for grilling	Sear for 1 minute on each side, Move to grill to finish cooking. 3 minutes a side for rare.
Kifta (3 ounces)	*Grilling:* Medium heat with direct fire.	Skewered. Grill 2 minutes per side turning 3-4 times. (Internal temp. 165° F)
Lamb Chops (6 oz. each)	*Grilling:* Medium heat with direct fire.	Marinate. Grill 4 minutes per side for rare. 6 minutes per side for medium rare.
Lamb, Leg (4 pounds)	*Rotisserie:* Medium heat with indirect fire. Covered cooking	Marinate. Cook 12 minutes per pound for med. rare.(internal temp. 135°)at 275° F. Allow to sit for 20 minutes before slicing.
Lobster Tail (5-6 oz. Tail)	*Grilling:* Medium heat, direct fire.	Remove tail meat from the shell and butterfly the tail. Place on the grill with butterflied side down first. Grill for 5-6 minutes per side.
London Broil (Flank Steak 1" thick)	*Grilling:* High heat for grill searing with direct fire. Medium heat direct fire for finish cooking.	Marinate: Overnight Cook 5-6 minutes each side for Med. rare. Allow to sit 10- 15 minutes before slicing.

Searing & Grilling Methods

Product	Method & Fire*	Cooking Time**
Pork, loin (Boneless) (3 pounds)	*Grilling & Roasting:* Medium heat indirect fire, covered cooking	Cook for 10 minutes per pound at 300° (Internal Temp. 165°F)
Pork, tenderloin (3 pounds)	*Grilling:* Medium heat direct fire, Low heat, direct fire, covered cooking	Cook for 3 minutes side Turn heat to low. (Internal Temp. 165°F)
Prime Rib Roast (5 pounds)	*Rotisserie:* Medium heat with indirect fire. Covered cooking.	Cook on spit, 15 minutes per pound for rare (internal temp. 135°) at 275° F Allow to sit 20 minutes before slicing.
Ribs, Spare & St. Louis Ribs (2 -3 pounds) membrane removed	*Grilling:* High heat, direct fire. Low heat, indirect fire. Covered Cooking.	Grill ribs (high) on the meat side 4 minutes, turn grill on bone side 4 minutes. Move to indirect heat and cook for 3-4 hours (250° F) until tender.
Ribs, Baby Back (1 1/2 pounds) membrane removed	*Grilling:* High heat, direct fire. Low heat, indirect fire. Covered Cooking.	Grill ribs (high) on the meat side 3 minutes, turn grill on bone side 3 minutes. Move to indirect heat and cook for 2-3 hours (250° F) until tender.
Salmon Fillets (8 oz. fillet 1" thick)	*Grilling:* Medium heat, direct	Grill on each side 4-5 minutes. fire. (Internal Temp. 165° F)

Searing & Grilling Methods

Product	Method & Fire*	Cooking Time**
Scallops (1" dia. Scallops)	*Grilling:* High heat, direct fire	Place scallops on the grill over direct fire. Grill for 4 minutes on each side.
Scallops (1" dia. Scallops)	*Griddle Searing:* High heat, direct fire using cast iron griddle. Low heat, direct fire.	Place scallops on lightly oiled griddle surface. Sear on each side for 3-4 minutes.
Scrod (8 ounce fillet)	*Roasting* High heat, indirect fire.	Place scrod fillet in aluminum roasting pan. Add a little water, drizzle with butter, cook covered for 10-12 minutes. (Internal Temp. 165° F)
Shrimp (16/20 ct. Shrimp)	*Grilling:* Medium Heat, direct fire.	Place shrimp on grill and cook for 4-5 minutes. Shrimp will turn pink when done.
Steaks (1" thick)	*Searing & Grilling:* High heat for searing with direct fire. Longer cooking times use indirect fire.	Sear 1 minute on each side. Then place over grill for finished cooking. 6 minutes on each side for med. rare
Swordfish Steaks (1" thick steaks)	*Grilling:* Medium heat, direct fire.	Grill on each side 4-5 minutes. (Internal Temp. 165° F)
Tenderloin, whole (5 pounds)	*Searing & Grilling:* High heat for searing. Medium heat for grill finish cooking. Covered cooking.	Sear for 1 minute on all sides and and ends of meat. Roast for 30 min. at 300°.

Product	Method & Fire*	Cooking Time**
Turkey Breast bone - in (5 lb.)	*Grilling & Roasting:* Medium heat, direct fire for grilling. Low heat, indirect fire for roasting. Covered cooking.	Grill breast skin over direct fire 6 minutes. Turn and grill for 6 minutes. Move over indirect heat and roast at 275° until internal temp. 185° F.
Turkey, whole 10-12 pound	*Rotisserie:* Medium heat, indirect fire. Covered cooking.	Center turkey on spit, cook at 300° (Internal Temp. 185° F) 10-12 minutes per pound.
Tuna Loin (2 pound whole loin)	*Searing & Roasting:* High heat, direct fire. Low heat, direct fire. (*Griddle sear for better flavor.*) Covered cooking.	Sear on all sides for 1 minute. Reduce heat and roast for 10-15 minutes. (Internal Temp. 165° F)
Veal Scaloppini (2 ounces each)	*Searing:* High heat with direct fire.	Sear and cook on each side for 2 minutes.

* For gas and charcoal grills, use the hand rule for checking the heat of the fire. (See Chapter 2: Fire & Fuel Basics.

** Cooking time will vary depending on weather conditions (temperature, rain, wind, etc.) and style of grill used.

***Roasting is used, after grilling, when longer cooking times are needed and indirect heat is required.

By using these simple guidelines along with your new understanding of cooking methods and grill functions, you will be on your way to a professional grilling experience.

Chapter 11
Rotisserie Dynamics

Rotisserie cooking will produce some of the BEST tasting products that you will ever eat. Let's start with the method itself. According to the American Heritage Dictionary the definition for rotisserie cooking is: "A cooking device equipped with a rotating spit on which meat or other food is roasted." It is as simple as that! The method takes longer than grilling, but less time than smoking. Rotisserie cooking is awesome for one main reason; the product self bastes. Because of the constant rotation, the product juices continue to roll around it's surface while it is cooking! This self basting method intensifies flavor, and most of all moisture!

Rotisserie attachments are available for most grills, whether they are charcoal or gas. Look for equipment that has a sturdy spit, holding prongs, and a motor strong enough to last and turn large pieces of meat. Better spits come the counter weights for balancing your product. Different types of baskets are available, including flat baskets for steaks and fish and round tumble baskets for vegetables.

Old fashioned spit roasting was the origination of the cook style that is today's rotisserie cooking. Large cuts of meat or whole carcass animals were skewered on a long straight sapling trunk or metal rod (spit) that would support the weight and take the heat of the fire. This mechanism was placed over a large coal bed of burned down wood (natural chunk charcoal) and rotated slowly by someone tending to the entire process.

Spit roasting was originally a direct radiant style of cooking, where the heat of the fire was intense, causing the meat to sear and self baste due to the rotation of the meat on the spit rod. As this process expanded, it evolved to modify and simplify the fight and time consumption that spit roasting required. Hoods were often added to help maintain a higher and more even heat source, lowering the cook time and increasing the moisture level of the food. Fires were moved out from under the food to minimize the burning or grease flare ups from a direct fire below the food. Spit supports were made with multiple slots or an adjustable height factor to assist in temperature control. Some or all of these concepts have been incorporated into today's modern equipment, to allow for a more controllable cooking process.

The application of heat (any fuel - gas or wood) for rotisserie cooking falls into four basic concepts that allow for the types of control mentioned above:

- **Heat below the food**

This concept has both intense radiant heat and a softer heat created by air convection, over the food, when placed above the fire. It is critical to have quick adjustability of food placement or heat intensity for this process to work.

- **Heat behind, or to the side of the food**

This concept of heat has one or both types of heat. It can be intense radiant heat off of a glowing infrared burner (not all back burners are infrared) and/or a softer heat by air convection around the food due to a hood trapping and creating a rotating convective air mass.

- **Single source, soft indirect heat below the food**

This concept of heat produced by an off set fire, has a varying intensity of radiant heat and a softer heat by air convection. A hood creates a rotating convective air mass around the food. The varying intensity of radiant heat is controlled by the distance between the fire and the food. The closer the fire the hotter the foods surface will be and a watchful eye is required.

- **Double source, indirect heat below the food**

This concept of heat, produced by using two smaller off set fires, has a stronger varying intensity of radiant heat and a softer heat by air

Rotisserie Dynamics

convection created by a hood trapping and creating a rotating convective air mass. The varying intensity of radiant heat is controlled by the distance between the fire and the food(doubled on two sides). The closer the fires the hotter the foods surface will be and the watchful eye is absolutely required here.

Mounting the food correctly onto the spit, is a precise action that can make or break the success of rotisserie cooking. If the food is trussed firmly, and mounted tightly between the forks, you have accomplished the basics. Next you need to start the motor turning, and listen/watch to see if the food is balanced on the spit. A poorly balanced spit will lead to the product cooking unevenly, and will put a huge strain on the motor causing improper rotation. When unbalanced, the heavy side will cause the food to slip, as the weight reaches the bottom of the rotation you will hear the motor strain. At this point visually mark the heavy side and turn off the motor. If you don't have a counterbalance weight, you must reposition the food on the axis of the spit and reposition the forks to find a balance. Repeat as necessary until the food rotates evenly without motor strain. With a counterbalance weight, you must move the weight to the opposite side of the foods heavy point that you visually marked. Now turn the motor on and see if you have properly placed the counter balance. Once you have it located properly you adjust the weight in and out from the axis of the spit to find the perfect balance. Repeat as necessary until the food rotates evenly without motor strain. You are now ready to start the grill fire, in preparation for cooking

Place a foil roasting pan under the product. The pan makes clean up faster, controls flare up caused by fat drippings, helps retain moisture while cooking, and most importantly, it catches juices and fat, that can be used to baste while cooking.

Since rotisserie cooking is a longer cooking method it is a great time to add wood smoke for extra flavor. Use the information you learned in Chapter 9, Special Cooking Tips.

Rotisserie cooking is as good as it gets, not only is the flavor of the food exceptional but the presentation is dynamic.

Chapter 12
Cleaning & Care of
Your Grill

There is nothing worse than uncovering your grill, opening the lid and seeing a dirty grill caked with food particles. A clean grill that has been properly cared for will last longer, is easier to use, and will lead to a pleasant and successful grilling experience.

Cleaning the grill

It is best to clean your grill after each use. When cleaning, always use the most mild cleaner first, then if necessary, use stronger cleaning agents. ie. if soap and water does the job don't use oven cleaner.

When you have finished cooking, turn the heat off, and let the grill cool down. (I let it cool while I am eating.) When using a charcoal grill, put the fire out by closing the air vents, allowing the charcoal to burn down and fall into the ash tray for easy clean up and removal.

Brush the food particles off both sides of the grill grate, top and bottom, with a brass bristle brush, that fits in between the rods. If you have a griddle remove charred remains with a scraper, then use the brass bristle brush. Once the grates and griddle are scrapped and brushed, wipe them down completely, with a clean cloth or paper towel. Spray them down with a light coating of high quality oil (ie. grape seed oil) or a food release product (ie. Pam) to protect the grates until the next grilling time. If you are going long periods of time between grilling, take care not to over oil the grates, since oil will turn rancid.

Wipe down the entire inside of the grill, with a soft cloth or paper towel, to remove excess dirt & grease, which can lead to off flavors and flare ups. The outside of the grill should be cleaned using a mild spray cleaner, to keep grease, finger prints and food from burning on the surface, making it increasingly difficult to clean.

To clean the outside stainless parts of a grill, use a recommended stainless steel cleaner, use only soft abrasive pads. Always scrub in the direction of the grain. **NEVER USE STEEL WOOL!**

Once a year remove all parts of the grill; cooking grates, heat deflectors, ash and drip pans, vaporizer plates or flame tamers, burners from gas grills and remove charcoal grates from charcoal grills. Wearing gloves, completely clean the inside grill surface, sides and top including the inside of hood, with a degreaser. You want to remove any excessive grease build up and food particles, for two reasons. First, excessive grease can lead to a fire hazard. Second, grease and food particles create a food safety hazard and off flavors in your cooked food. Make sure that grates and griddles are rinsed well to remove the degreasing agent. Wipe down the top and sides or hose the grill down lightly with clean water to remove the dirt and cleaning agent.

Once the grill is rinsed cleaned, allow it to dry thoroughly before covering or storing. All grills, whether gas or coal, need to be covered after each use and during long storage times. I also recommend, if you are not grilling during the winter months, that you store your grill out of the weather elements.

Helpful Hint: After cleaning a gas grill, the parts can be dried in the grill, by turning the burners on low heat for a few minutes.

Vaporizers & Flame Tamer s
Washing after every use is not necessary, we suggest that you use a brass bristle brush to remove stubborn burnt on cooking residue, and build up of any sauces, seasonings or grease.

Ceramic Briquettes
Ceramic briquettes need cleaned, if grease can be seen on the

briquettes or if you get frequent flare up during cooking. To clean briquettes, light the grill and let it burn on high for about 30 minutes. Note: make sure to check with the manufacturers directions.

Burner Tubes (Venturi Tubes) and Burners

Regularly check openings of venturi tubes and burners for insects (spiders, ants, wasps). this check will reduce the chance of a flash-back or back burn caused by insects that periodically, particularly in late summer or early fall , build webs and nest in the openings. These blockages are dangerous and must be cleaned out. Use a venturi brush made especially for this job or a bottle brush. Never use pesticides or chemicals. Cleaning burners prolongs there life. Using a Brass Bristle brush the clean the entire outer surface of each burner to remove loose corrosion. Shine a flashlight through the main burner opening to check for clogged ports (flame holes). Clean clogged ports with a stiff wire, open paper clips work for this. Inspect burners for any opening or crack caused by corrosion, replace damaged burners immediately. Burners should be cleaned every six months, more often for heavy use. They may be cleaned with soap & water, but drying by lighting each burner is a must to minimize rust and corrosion.
Note: make sure to check with the manufacturers directions.

Drip Tray

If you line the drip tray with foil it will be easier to clean, just fold up the foil and discard, then wash it with mild detergent and warm water. You may need to use a degreaser. It is important to change the foil regularly, excessive fat and grease caught in the tray, can go rancid or catch on fire. After cleaning, always make sure the drip tray is back in the proper position.

HELPFUL HINTS: Fill the tray with a thin layer of clay cat liter (the old fashioned kind with no additives), sand or some other non combustible, absorbent material.

Caring for Stainless Steel Grill Grates

A light wipe or spray of oil before cooking will help food resist sticking. Scrub stainless steel grill grates immediately after you finish cooking and turn the flame off. Wear a mitt to protect your hands from heat and steam. A brass bristle brush and plain water do a fine job of removing food particles. Dip the brush frequently in water then scrub a section of the grate, repeat until the entire grate is clean. If the grates are extremely dirty, you may remove the grates when cool and clean them with soap and hot water , then rinse until soap is removed.

Caring for Porcelain Grill Grates

As with stainless steel grates a light wipe or spray of oil before cooking will help the food resist sticking. Clean cooled grates after each use, using mild soap and warm water, with a nylon or brass bristle brush. Be careful not to chip porcelain grates by dropping or hitting them with hard objects or using heavy metal cooking utensils.

Caring For Cast Iron Grill Grates

To help preserve uncoated (raw) cast iron cooking surfaces and to minimize rusting and sticking, cooking grills and griddles should be properly seasoned before use. Seasoning is the process of allowing oil to be absorbed into the iron, which creates a natural non-stick, rustproof finish. It is a very simple process.

First Seasoning:

Remove the cast iron surfaces from the grill and wash them thoroughly with mild dish washing liquid and dry immediately, do not allow to drain dry. Coat the entire surface, top and bottom with a generous layer of lard, grape seed oil, or peanut oil. Do not use salted fats such as butter, margarine or flavored oils for seasoning. Heat grill to approximately 350° F to 385° F, adding more lard or oil as needed until dry spots disappear. After 30 minutes, turn all burners off and allow your grill to cool completely. Once cooled, reapply another light coating of lard or oil. The cooking grills are now seasoned and ready to use.

The cooking surface should be oiled frequently, or as dry spots develop, to prevent rust. If rust does occur, clean with a brass bristle brush and repeat the seasoning process. In a marine environment more frequent seasoning may be required. The more the grill is used the easier it will be to maintain the cooking surface and the less likely it is to rust.

Cleaning you grill after every use will lead to a better grilling experience every time, and when well cared for, will maintain proper function and appearance for years to come.

Let's Get it Going Starters

Fajita Quesadillas

(Beef or Chicken)
4 portions

Ingredients:

1 lb.	Beef Flank or Chicken Breast
1 TB.	Lemon Pepper
1 cup	Fajita Marinade (p.98)
4 ea.	12" Flour Tortillas, warm
3/4 cup	Red & Yellow Peppers, cleaned, seeded, cut in strips.
3/4 cup	Green Peppers, cleaned, seeded, cut in strips.
1 cup	White Onion, peeled, cut in half and thinly sliced.
4 oz.	Cheddar Cheese, grated
1/2 cup	Fresh Tomatoes, diced
4 TB.	Scallions, fresh, thinly sliced

Heat Source:
Direct fire, medium heat (reference pg. 7-10)

Preparation:
Trim flank steak or chicken of any excess fat. Season the beef or chicken with lemon pepper and place in a clean container. Pour the fajita marinade over the meat and marinade for at least 6 hours.

Turn grill on and while grill is heating, remove the meat from the marinade. When ready to grill place the meat on the grill and grill on both sides of the meat. While the meat is grilling, heat the solid griddle side of the grill on medium heat. Once the meat is cooked, slice the meat across the grain about 1/4" thick. Prepare the peppers and onions and grill on the grill using a grill screen or pan. Cook until al dente (halfway). Set aside and hold warm.

Place a little bit of salad oil on the griddle and coat the surface evenly. Place a flour tortilla on the grill and sprinkle cheddar cheese over the whole tortilla. Place 1/4 of the peppers and onions to one side, top with 1/4 of the sliced meat. Top the meat with diced tomatoes and diced scallions. Fold the other side of the tortilla over the filled side, flatten lightly with a spatula and grill crisp on one side, turning to grill crisp on the other side.

Remove from the griddle, place on cutting board and cut into 4 equal triangles.

Approximate Cooking Time: 10-15 minutes

Let's Get Going Starters

Baba Ghanough w/ Grilled Pita

(Eggplant Dip)
about 2 quarts

Ingredients:

5 pounds	*Whole Fresh Eggplants, washed*
2 TB.	*Garlic, fresh , minced*
4 TB.	*Kosher Salt*
3 cups	*Tahini Paste*
2 cups	*Fresh Lemon Juice*

Heat Source:
Direct fire, medium heat then low heat (reference pg. 7-10)

Preparation:
Pierce the eggplant with a knife and cook on the grill using medium high heat, turning once, until charred and tender. Cook eggplant until very soft on low heat. Cool completely. Cut the eggplant in half and scoop out the flesh, discarding juice and excess seeds. Mash the pulp.

Mash the garlic until puree form. Add garlic and salt to the eggplant, stirring to mix well.

Add the tahini and lemon juice a little at a time to taste. Adjust seasonings and chilled until needed.

Approximate Cooking Time: 10-15 minutes

To Serve:
Drizzle with olive oil.

Special Note:
This special recipe was taught to me by Peggy Haddad.

Grape & Brie Quesadillas

4 each

Ingredients:

4 ea.	*8" Flour Tortillas*
4 TB.	*Melted Butter*
8 ounce	*Brie Cheese, rind removed*
1 cup	*Red Grapes, seedless, cut in half*
4 TB.	*Pecans, pieces*

Heat Source:
Direct fire, medium heat (reference pg. 7-10)

Preparation:
Sliced the brie into 8 very thin slices. Cut all the grapes into halves.

On medium high heat, heat the flat griddle part of your grill or a flat cast iron pan.

Brush the flour tortillas on one side with the melted butter and place onto the warm griddle, buttered side down.

Immediately, lay the slices of brie cheese on one half of the tortilla, top the cheese with the slices grapes and pecan pieces.

Fold the other half of the flour tortilla over the cheese, grape and pecan half. Lightly press the tortilla together and grill golden brown on both sides.

Remove from the griddle and cut each quesadilla into 4 triangles.

Approximate Cooking Time: 8-10 minutes

Special Note:
Serve with sliced fruits, i.e. pears, melons, apples

Beef Satay

4 orders

Ingredients:

1 pound	*Beef Flank Steak, sliced thin*
1 cup	*Onions, white, peeled, rough chop*
1 TB.	*Garlic, fresh*
3 TB.	*Cumin, ground*
3 TB.	*Coriander, ground*
1 TB.	*Salt & Pepper 50/50*
4 TB.	*Curry Powder*
1 tsp.	*Turmeric*
2 cups	*Olive Oil*

Heat Source:
Direct fire, high heat (reference pg. 7-10)

Preparation:
Sliced the flank steak into 1/4" thin 5" long strips. Lightly flatten the meat with a meat mallet. Place in a flat glass or stainless pan.

Puree the onions in a cuisinart. Combine all the ingredients and place over low heat for 20 minutes. Cool down completely before using for marinating beef satay.

Once cooled down, pour over the meat and allow to marinate for at least 12 hours. Tossing a couple of times to coat all the meat well.

After meat has marinated, remove and drain well. Weave the strips onto 8" bamboo skewers, that have been soaked in water for about an hour.

Heat the grill to a high heat. Lightly oil the grill before placing the skewered meat onto the grill. Sear the satay on both sides and remove from the grill. Meat will only take about 2 minutes per side.

Approximate Cooking Time: 4-5 minutes

To Serve:
Drizzle with soy sauce topped with thinly sliced scallions and serve warm.

Mini Crabcakes with Chili Aioli Sauce

4 orders - 8 crabcakes

Ingredients:

1/2 cup	Mayonnaise
1 ea.	Whole Egg
1 tsp.	Old Bay Seasoning
1/2 tsp.	Black Pepper, fine grind
1/2 tsp.	Dry Mustard, ground
pinch	Salt
2 tsp.	Lemon Juice, fresh
1 TB.	Parsley, chopped
4 TB.	Roasted Red Peppers, jarred, fine chopped
3/4 cup	White Bread Crumbs
1 pound	Blue Crab Meat, fresh

Heat Source:
Direct fire, medium heat (reference pg. 7-10)

Preparation:
Combine all ingredients, except the bread crumbs and crab meat, together in a bowl and mix well. Add the crab meat and fold gently into the mixture. Add the bread crumbs until the mixture comes together and holds together. Chill completely. Once chilled, form into 2 ounce crabcakes, flattened slightly until about 1/4" thick.

Using medium heat, warm the griddle or flat cast iron griddle until hot. Lightly oil the griddle to prevent the cakes from sticking. Cook the crab cakes golden brown on both sides. Serve with Aioli Sauce.

Approximate Cooking Time: 8-10 minutes

Chili Aioli Sauce: (about 1 cup)

3/4 cup	Mayonnaise
1 TB.	Whole Grain Mustard
1 tsp.	Minced Jalapeno Peppers
1 tsp.	Minced Garlic
1/2 tsp.	Chili Powder
1 TB.	Cilantro, minced
1 tsp.	Lime Juice
2 tsp.	Cider Vinegar
to taste	Kosher Salt

Combine all ingredients together and blend well. Chill before serving with crab cakes.

Let's Get Going Starters

Cheese & Salsa Quesadillas

4 each

Ingredients:

4 ea.	*8" Flour Tortillas, warm*
4 oz.	*Cheddar Cheese, grated*
8 TB.	*Salsa, your favorite*
4 TB.	*Scallions, fresh, thinly sliced*
4 TB.	*Jalapenos, sliced thin*

Heat Source:
Direct fire, medium heat (reference pg. 7-10)

Preparation:
On medium heat the flat griddle part of your grill or a flat cast iron pan.

Brush the flour tortillas on one side with the melted butter and place onto the warm griddle, buttered side down.

Immediately, evenly divide the grated cheese between the tortillas, top the cheese with the salsa, scallions and sliced jalapenos.

Fold the other half of the flour tortilla over the cheese, salsa, scallion and jalapeno half. Lightly press the tortilla together and grill golden brown on both sides.

Remove from the griddle and cut each quesadilla into 4 triangles.

Approximate Cooking Time: 4-5 minutes

BBQ Chicken Quesadillas

4 portions

Ingredients:

1 lb.	*BBQ Chicken Breast, cooked & diced*
4 ea.	*12" Flour Tortillas, warm*
1/4 cup	*BBQ Sauce, your favorite*
4 oz.	*White Onion, peeled, cut in half and thinly sliced.*
4 oz.	*Smoked Cheddar Cheese, grated*
4 oz.	*Fresh Tomatoes, diced*
4 TB.	*Scallions, fresh, thinly sliced*

Heat Source:
Direct fire, medium heat (reference pg. 7-10)

Preparation:
Dice the cooked barbecued chicken.

Heat the solid griddle side of the grill on medium heat.

Place a little bit of salad oil on the griddle and coat the surface evenly. place a flour tortilla on the grill and sprinkle cheddar cheese over the whole tortilla.

Top the cheese with the diced chicken, white onion, fresh tomatoes and sliced scallions. Top all the ingredients with 2 ounces of BBQ sauce.

Fold the tortilla over in half , press together lightly. Cook until golden brown on both sides.

Remove from the griddle, place on cutting board and cut into 4 equal triangles.

Approximate Cooking Time: 8-10 minutes

Crab Stuffed Mushrooms

4 portions

Ingredients:

16 each	*Fresh Mushroom Caps, silver dollar size*
1/2 batch	*Crabcake Recipe (p. 61)*
1/2 cup	*Chili Aoili Sauce (p. 61)*

Heat Source:
Direct fire, low heat (reference pg. 7-10)
Indirect fire, medium heat (reference pg. 7-10)

Preparation:
Remove the stems from the mushrooms and wash the mushroom caps, removing any dirt. After washing the mushrooms, turn them with the cavity side down on some paper towels, to absorb the excess moisture.

Heat the solid griddle side of the grill on low heat. With the other side of the grill on medium heat.

Stuff the mushroom caps with the crabcake mixture, dividing the crab mixture equally.

Place the stuffed mushroom caps on the low heat griddle side of your grill or a flat cast iron skillet. Close the lid on the grill and roast for until mushrooms are hot and golden brown.

Remove the mushrooms and place on a serving platter, topped with the chili aioli sauce.

Approximate Cooking Time: 10-15 minutes

Special note:
This item lends itself well to being cooked on a plank, for that lightly smoky flavor. Place the plank over the heat until it begins to smoke. Place the mushrooms on the plank, and place the plank on the low heat side and finish cooking until mushrooms are done, leaving the indirect heat going.

Gorgonzola Stuffed Mushrooms

4 portions

Ingredients:

16 each	*Fresh Mushroom Caps, silver dollar size*
1/4 cup	*Sun dried Tomato Pesto*
2 ounces	*Gorgonzola Cheese, crumbled*

Heat Source:
Indirect fire, medium heat (reference pg. 7-10)

Preparation:
Remove the stems from the mushrooms and wash the mushroom caps, removing any dirt. After washing the mushrooms, turn them with the cavity side down on some paper towels, to absorb the excess moisture.

Preheat one side of the grill. Using indirect heat method.

When dried, fill the cavity of the mushroom cap with 1 teaspoon of the Sun dried Tomato Pesto. Top with a small amount of Gorgonzola cheese. Place on the no heat side of grill. Close the lid and cook the mushrooms 15 minutes. Just until cheese starts to melt and filling is warm.

Approximate Cooking Time: 10-15 minutes

Sun dried Tomato Pesto (2 cups)

1 jar	*Sun dried Tomatoes, in oil, 12 ounce*
1/2 cup	*Garlic, fresh, peeled*
1 cup	*Walnuts, chopped*
1/3 cup	*Sage, fresh, chopped*
8 ounces	*Parmesan Cheese, grated*
1 cup	*Olive Oil*
Salt	*to taste*
Pepper	*to taste*

Place everything in a cuisinart except the Olive oil, salt, pepper and parmesan cheese. When finely chopped mix in the remaining ingredients, blend until well mix. Hold in refrigerator for use and freeze leftover product.

Let's Get Going Starters

Steamed Mussels

4 -6 people

Ingredients:

4 pounds	*Mussels, cleaned and washed*
1 quart	*White Wine Clam Broth*
4 ounces	*Melted Butter, unsalted*
1/2 cup	*Red Onion, minced*
1/4 cup	*Fresh Parsley, finely chopped*

Heat Source:

Direct fire, high heat (reference pg. 7-10)

Preparation:

Preheat the grill on high heat. Wash and clean the mussels and place in shallow roasting pan. Add the white wine broth and the minced red onion. Cover the roasting pan with foil and seal tight. Place the covered roasting pan on the high heat and allow the broth to come to a boil. Reduce the heat to low and cook the mussels until they "pop" open.

Remove the mussels from the heat, uncover and add the melted butter and chopped parsley to the mussels, stirring the mussels, to ensure that they are all open and cooked. Discard any mussels that did not open.

Place the mussels in a warm serving bowl and pour the broth with the butter, onions and parsley over the mussels. Serve with warm french bread or garlic bread.

Approximate Cooking Time: 6-8 minutes

White Wine Broth (1 quart)

3 cups	*Clam Juice, fresh, jarred or canned*
1 cup	*White Wine, chardonnay*
1/4 cup	*Garlic, fresh, fine chopped*

Peel and chop the fresh garlic. In a container, add the clam juice, white wine and fresh garlic together. Stir to mix well. Hold chilled until needed.

Pesto Bruschetta with Red & Yellow Tomatoes

4 -6 people

Ingredients:

1 loaf	*French Bread, baguette*
2 cups	*Basil Pesto*
4 ounces	*Parmesan Cheese, finely shredded*
2 cups	*Red & Yellow Tomatoes, chilled (p. 191)*

Heat Source:
Direct fire, low heat (reference pg. 7-10)

Preparation:
Preheat the grill with low heat.

Slice the french baguette on the bias, cutting the slices about 1/2" thick. Spread one side of the slices with the pesto sauce. Spread all the slices before going to the grill. These slices grill very fast and you want to be quick so that the bruschetta does not burn.

Place the slices on the grill with the pesto side down first. Turn the slices over and grill on the plain side to toast the slices. Do not allow the slices and pesto to burn. Top the pesto side of the bruschetta with the shredded parmesan cheese. Remove the bruschetta from the grill and place on a warm platter.

Place the balsamic tomatoes in a bowl and serve in the center of the of the bruschetta.

Approximate Cooking Time: 2-3 minutes

Basil Pesto (2 cups)

8 ounces	*Fresh Basil Leaves*
3 TB.	*Garlic, fresh, peeled*
1/4 cup	*Walnuts or Pine Nuts, chopped*
2 ounces	*Parmesan Cheese, grated*
1/2 cup	*Olive Oil*
Salt	*to taste*
Pepper	*to taste*

Place everything in a cuisinart except the Olive oil, salt, pepper and parmesan cheese. When finely chopped mix in the remaining ingredients, blend until well mix. Hold in refrigerator for use and freeze leftover product.

Let's Get Going Starters

Chicken Satay

4 orders

Ingredients:

1 pound	Chicken Tenders, flattened
1 cup	Onions, white, peeled, rough chop
1 TB.	Garlic, fresh
3 TB.	Cumin, ground
3 TB.	Coriander, ground
1 TB.	Salt & Pepper 50/50
4 TB.	Curry Powder
1 tsp.	Turmeric
2 cups	Olive Oil

Heat Source:
Direct fire, high heat (reference pg. 7-10)

Preparation:
Flatten the tenders into 1/4" thin 5" long strips. Place in a flat glass or stainless pan.

Puree the onions in a cuisinart. Combine all the ingredients and place over low heat for 20 minutes. Cool down completely before using for marinating beef satay.

Once cooled down, pour over the meat and allow to marinate for at least 12 hours. Tossing a couple of times to coat all the meat well.

After meat has marinated, remove and drain well. Weave the strips onto 8" bamboo skewers, that have been soaked in water for about an hour.

Heat the grill to a high heat. Lightly oil the grill before placing the skewered meat onto the grill. Sear the satay on both sides and remove from the grill. Meat will only need to cook about 2 minutes a side.

Approximate Cooking Time: 4-5 minutes

To Serve:
Mix 4 tablespoons soy sauce, 2 tablespoons of sesame seed oil, 1 tablespoon of peanut butter. Drizzle the mixture over the warm grilled chicken. Top with finely chopped peanuts and thinly sliced scallions.

Deviled Grilled Shrimp

4 orders

Ingredients:

16 each	*Large Shrimp (16/20 ct.), peeled and cleaned*
1 cup	*Louisiana Hot Sauce*
1/2 cup	*Liquid Margarine*
1/4 cup	*White Vinegar*
1/4 cup	*Barbecue Sauce*
1 tsp.	*Black Pepper, fine grind*

Heat Source:
Direct fire, medium heat (reference pg. 7-10)

Preparation:
After cleaning the shrimp, skewer them on a soaked bamboo skewer, placing four shrimp on each skewer.

Combine all the the remaining ingredients together in a bowl. After skewering all the shrimp place them in a shallow pan and pour the marinade over the shrimp cover them completely. Place the shrimp in the refrigerator for at least 4 hours. Turn several times to insure proper marinating.

Preheat the grill with medium heat. While the grill is preheating remove the shrimp from the refrigerator and drain the shrimp from the marinade. Marinade may thicken while under refrigeration, allowing them to sit at room temperature will allow the marinade to warm slightly. Remove any excessive marinade from the shrimp before grilling. Save the marinade for basting the shrimp while they are grilling.

Lightly oil the grates of the grill before placing the shrimp on the grill. Grill the shrimp on each side for 3-4 minutes. Once you have turned the shrimp, baste them with the marinade while they finish grilling.

Remove from the grill and serve.

Approximate Cooking Time: 6-8 minutes

Who Needs an Oven! Cracker Crust Pizzas

BBQ Chicken Pizza

1-10" pizza

Ingredients:

1 each	*10 inch Flour Tortilla*
2 ounce	*Rib Stars™ Double "J" BBQ Sauce (p. 163)*
	or your favorite
1 1/2 ounces	*Mozzarella Cheese, shredded*
1 ounces	*Yellow Cheddar Cheese, shredded*
4 ounces	*Grilled Chicken Breast, diced*
1/4 cup	*Red Onion, thin sliced rings*
1 ounce	*Scallions, diced*
1 TB.	*Parsley, fresh, chopped*

Heat Source:
Direct fire, low heat and then high heat (reference pg. 7-10)
Indirect fire, medium heat (reference pg. 7-10)

Preparation:
Pizzas are best done on the flat griddle, either on gas or use a 10" flat cast iron griddle for live coal grills. Use a medium heat for grilling. If using a gas grill, set the grate side to medium heat and the flat griddle side to low heat for preheating.

Place the flour tortilla on the griddle and toast on the one side. Flip the tortilla over when crisp on the bottom side. Top the tortilla with the barbecue sauce, spreading around the whole tortilla, leaving about 1/4" ring at the outer edge of the tortilla. Top the sauce with the two cheeses, placing the white cheese down first, top the cheeses with the diced chicken, red onions and diced scallions. Turn the heat on the griddle side to high and shut the lid of the grill and finishing cooking until the tortilla bottom is crisp and the toppings are warm and bubble. Pizza takes about 5 minutes after topping.

Remove from the fire, garnish the top with the chopped parsley and cut into 8 wedges.

Approximate Cooking Time: 6-8 minutes

Special Note:
Pizza can also be made with a ready made precooked pizza dough (thick or thin).

Cracker Crust Pizzas

Pesto Pizza
1-10" pizza

Ingredients:
1 each	*10 inch Flour Tortilla*
2 ounce	*Basil Pesto (p.67)*
2 ounces	*Mozzarella Cheese, shredded*
1 ounces	*Parmesan Cheese, shredded*
1 TB.	*Basil, fresh, chopped*

Heat Source:
Direct fire, low heat and then high heat (reference pg. 7-10)
Indirect fire, medium heat (reference pg. 7-10)

Preparation:
Pizzas are best done on the flat griddle, either on gas or use a 10" flat cast iron griddle for live coal grills. Use a medium heat for grilling. If using a gas grill, set the grate side to medium heat and the flat griddle side to low heat for preheating.

Place the flour tortilla on the griddle and toast on the one side. Flip the tortilla over when crisp on the bottom side. Top the tortilla with the pesto sauce, spreading around the whole tortilla, leaving about 1/4" ring at the outer edge of the tortilla. Top the pesto with the mozzarella first and then the parmesan. Turn the heat on the griddle side to high and shut the lid of the grill and finishing cooking until the tortilla bottom is crisp and the toppings are warm and bubble. Pizza takes about 5 minutes after topping.

Remove from the fire, garnish the top with the chopped parsley and cut into 8 wedges.

Approximate Cooking Time: 6-8 minutes

Special Note:
Pizza can also be made with a ready made precooked pizza dough (thick or thin).

Grilled Vidalia Onion & Pepperoni Pizza

1-10" pizza

Ingredients:

1 each	*10 inch Flour Tortilla*
2 ounce	*Pizza Sauce, your favorite*
2 ounces	*Mozzarella Cheese, shredded*
1 ounces	*Parmesan Cheese, shredded*
1/4 cup	*Vadalia Onions, sliced thin, grilled*
1 ounces	*Pepperoni, sliced thin*

Heat Source:
Direct fire, low heat and then high heat (reference pg. 7-10)
Indirect fire, medium heat (reference pg. 7-10)

Preparation:
Pizzas are best done on the flat griddle, either on gas or use a 10" flat cast iron griddle for live coal grills. Use a medium heat for grilling. If using a gas grill, set the grate side to medium heat and the flat griddle side to low heat for preheating.

Place the flour tortilla on the griddle and toast on the one side. Flip the tortilla over when crisp on the bottom side. Top the tortilla with the pizza sauce, spreading around the whole tortilla, leaving about 1/4" ring at the outer edge of the tortilla. Top the sauce with the mozzarella first then the parmesan, grilled onions and pepperoni. Turn the heat on the griddle side to high and shut the lid of the grill and finishing cooking until the tortilla bottom is crisp and the toppings are warm and bubble. Pizza takes about 5 minutes after topping.

Remove from the fire and cut into 8 wedges.

Approximate Cooking Time: 6-8 minutes

Special Note:
Pizza can also be made with a ready made precooked pizza dough (thick or thin).

Grilled Vadalia Onions:

3 ounces	*Sliced Vadalia Onions, thin*
1 tsp.	*Granulated Sugar*

Using a grill pan, place the onions in the pan, sprinkle with the sugar, and grill sauté, until onions are just turning tender and slightly golden brown. Remove from the heat and use on the pizza.

Cracker Crust Pizzas

Garlic & Three Cheese Pizza

1-10" pizza

Ingredients:

1 each	10 inch Flour Tortilla
1 ounces	Olive Oil
1 tsp.	Crushed Red Pepper Flakes
1 TB.	Garlic, fresh, minced
2 ounces	Mozzarella Cheese, shredded
1 ounce	Parmesan Cheese, shredded
1 TB.	Oregano Leaves, dry

Heat Source:
Direct fire, low heat and then high heat (reference pg. 7-10)
Indirect fire, medium heat (reference pg. 7-10)

Preparation:
Pizzas are best done on the flat griddle, either on gas or use a 10" flat cast iron griddle for live coal grills. Use a medium heat for grilling. If using a gas grill, set the grate side to medium heat and the flat griddle side to low heat for preheating.

Place the flour tortilla on the griddle and toast on the one side. Flip the tortilla over when crisp on the bottom side. Brush the tortilla with the olive oil around the whole tortilla, leaving about 1/4" ring at the outer edge of the tortilla. Sprinkle the olive oil with the red pepper flakes and minced garlic. Top the sauce with the mozzarella first and then the parmesan. Turn the heat on the griddle side to high and shut the lid of the grill and finishing cooking until the tortilla bottom is crisp and the toppings are warm and bubble. Pizza takes about 5 minutes after topping.

Remove from the fire, garnish the top with the oregano. and cut into 8 wedges.

Approximate Cooking Time: 6-8 minutes

Special Note:
Pizza can also be made with a ready made precooked pizza dough (thick or thin).

Spiced Shrimp & Scallop Pizza

1-10" pizza

Ingredients:

1 each	10 inch Flour Tortilla
2 ounce	Rib Stars™ Hawg's Breath BBQ Sauce (p. 164)
2 ounces	Mozzarella Cheese, shredded
1 ounces	Parmesan Cheese, shredded
1 each	Roma Tomatoes, sliced into 10 slices
2 ounces	Spiced Grilled Shrimp, rough chopped
2 ounces	Spiced Grilled Scallops, rough chopped
1 TB.	Scallions, diced
as needed	Blackened Seasoning (p. 115)

Heat Source:

Direct fire, low heat and then high heat (reference pg. 7-10)
Indirect fire, medium heat (reference pg. 7-10)

Preparation:

Pizzas are best done on the flat griddle, either on gas or use a 10" flat cast iron griddle for live coal grills. Use a medium heat for grilling. If using a gas grill, set the grate side to medium heat and the flat griddle side to low heat for preheating.

Season the shrimp and scallops with blackened seasoning and cook on the grill until just cooked. Do not over cook. Remove the fire and rough chop.

Place the flour tortilla on the griddle and toast on the one side. Flip the tortilla over when crisp on the bottom side. Top the tortilla with the barbecue sauce, spreading around the whole tortilla, leaving about 1/4" ring at the outer edge of the tortilla. Top the sauce with the mozzarella first and then the parmesan. Top the cheeses with the sliced romas, diced seafood and sliced scallions. Turn the heat on the griddle side to high and shut the lid of the grill and finishing cooking until the tortilla bottom is crisp and the toppings are warm and bubble. Pizza takes about 5 minutes after topping.

Remove from the fire and cut into 8 wedges.

Approximate Cooking Time: 6-8 minutes

Special Note:

Pizza can also be made with a ready made precooked pizza dough (thick or thin).

Cracker Crust Pizzas

Margherita Pizza

1-10" pizza

Ingredients:

1 each	*10 inch Flour Tortilla*
1 ounce	*Olive Oil*
3 TB.	*Basil Pesto (p.67)*
2 ounces	*Mozzarella Cheese, shredded*
1 ounces	*Parmesan Cheese, shredded*
1 each	*Roma Tomatoes, cut into 10 slices*
1 TB.	*Basil, fresh, chopped*

Heat Source:
Direct fire, low heat and then high heat (reference pg. 7-10)
Indirect fire, medium heat (reference pg. 7-10)

Preparation:
Pizzas are best done on the flat griddle, either on gas or use a 10" flat cast iron griddle for live coal grills. Use a medium heat for grilling. If using a gas grill, set the grate side to medium heat and the flat griddle side to low heat for preheating.

Place the flour tortilla on the griddle and toast on the one side. Flip the tortilla over when crisp on the bottom side. Brush the tortilla with the olive oil, spread the pesto around the whole tortilla, leaving about 1/4" ring at the outer edge of the tortilla. Top the pesto with the mozzarella first and then the parmesan. Lay the sliced roma tomatoes around the pizza. Turn the heat on the griddle side to high and shut the lid of the grill and finish cooking until the tortilla bottom is crisp and the toppings are warm and bubble. Pizza takes about 5 minutes after topping.

Remove from the fire, garnish the top with the chopped basil and cut into 8 wedges.

Approximate Cooking Time: 6-8 minutes

Special Note:
Pizza can also be made with a ready made precooked pizza dough (thick or thin).

Nostra Pizza
1-10" pizza

Ingredients:

1 each	*10 inch Flour Tortilla*
2 ounce	*Pizza Sauce, your favorite*
2 ounces	*Mozzarella Cheese, shredded*
1 ounces	*Parmesan Cheese, shredded*
1 tsp.	*Oregano Leaves, dried*
1 1/2 ounces	*Roasted Red Peppers, jarred, cut into thin strips*
2 ounces	*Sweet Italian Sausage, precooked*
1 TB.	*Basil, fresh, chopped*

Heat Source:
Direct fire, low heat and then high heat (reference pg. 7-10)
Indirect fire, medium heat (reference pg. 7-10)

Preparation:
Pizzas are best done on the flat griddle, either on gas or use a 10" flat cast iron griddle for live coal grills. Use a medium heat for grilling. If using a gas grill, set the grate side to medium heat and the flat griddle side to low heat for preheating.

Place the flour tortilla on the griddle and toast on the one side. Flip the tortilla over when crisp on the bottom side. Brush the tortilla with the olive oil, top with the pizza sauce around the whole tortilla, leaving about 1/4" ring at the outer edge of the tortilla. Top the sauce with the mozzarella first and then the parmesan. Sprinkle the oregano over the cheeses, top with the sliced roasted red peppers and cooked sausage. Turn the heat on the griddle side to high and shut the lid of the grill and finishing cooking until the tortilla bottom is crisp and the toppings are warm and bubble. Pizza takes about 5 minutes after topping.

Remove from the fire, garnish the top with the chopped basil and cut into 8 wedges.

Approximate Cooking Time: 6-8 minutes

Special Note:
Pizza can also be made with a ready made precooked pizza dough (thick or thin) .

Chicken Pesto Pizza

1-10" pizza

Ingredients:

1 each	*10 inch Flour Tortilla*
1 ounce	*Olive Oil*
3 TB.	*Basil Pesto (p.67)*
2 ounces	*Mozzarella Cheese, shredded*
1 ounces	*Parmesan Cheese, shredded*
4 ounces	*Grilled Chicken Breast, diced*
1 each	*Roma Tomatoes, cut into 10 slices*
1 TB.	*Basil, fresh, chopped*

Heat Source:

Direct fire, low heat and then high heat (reference pg. 7-10)
Indirect fire, medium heat (reference pg. 7-10)

Preparation:

Pizzas are best done on the flat griddle, either on gas or use a 10" flat cast iron griddle for live coal grills. Use a medium heat for grilling. If using a gas grill, set the grate side to medium heat and the flat griddle side to low heat for preheating.

Place the flour tortilla on the griddle and toast on the one side. Flip the tortilla over when crisp on the bottom side. Brush the tortilla with the olive oil, spread the pesto around the whole tortilla, leaving about 1/4" ring at the outer edge of the tortilla. Top the pesto with the mozzarella first and then the parmesan. Top with the grilled diced chicken. Lay the sliced roma tomatoes around the pizza. Turn the heat on the griddle side to high and shut the lid of the grill and finishing cooking until the tortilla bottom is crisp and the toppings are warm and bubble. Pizza takes about 5 minutes after topping.

Remove from the fire, garnish the top with the chopped basil and cut into 8 wedges.

Approximate Cooking Time: 6-8 minutes

Special Note:

Pizza can also be made with a ready made precooked pizza dough (thick or thin).

Not Meant for the Refrigerator Grilled Salads

Grilled Caesar

2 entree salads

Ingredients:

1 each	*Romaine Lettuce Head*
3 ounces	*Caesar Dressing, your favorite*
2 ounces	*Croutons*
1 ounce	*Parmesan Cheese, shredded*

Heat Source:
Direct fire, medium heat (reference pg. 7-10)

Preparation:
Heat grill to medium heat. Lightly oil the grates before placing the romaine heads on the grill.

Clean the romaine head of any damaged outer leaves, then cut in half the long way, leaving the core intact, to hold the salad together when grilling. Wash and dry well before grilling.

Place the romaine on the grill cut side down and grill until the cut side is grilled and slightly wilted. You are only grilling the cut side of the romaine.

Remove the lettuce from the grill and immediately, top with the dressing, croutons and parmesan cheese. Serve Immediately!

Approximate Cooking Time: 3-4 minutes

Special Note:
This is a Great Twist to the normal cold caesar and easy to do. A fresh grinding of Black pepper will finish this salad.

Refreshing Char Grilled Chicken Salad

2 entree salads

Ingredients:

2 ounces	Spinach Leaves, fresh, whole
1/2 cup	Red Pepper, diced 1" cubes
1/2 cup	Celery, 1/2" bias sliced
1/2 cup	Carrots, julienne or shredded
2 cups	Cantaloupe, peeled, 1" diced cubes
2 each	Chicken Breast, 6 ounce, skinless, boneless, marinated in Italian dressing for 2 hours
4 ounces	Sesame Dressing
as needed	Sesame Seeds

Heat Source:
Direct fire, high heat (reference pg. 7-10)

Preparation:
Heat grill to high heat. Lightly oil the grates before grilling the chicken breast. Drain the breast from the marinade before grilling.

Prepare the red peppers, celery, carrots and cantaloupe. Wash the spinach and dry well before making the salads. Place half the spinach leaves on a 10" round plate, fanning the leaves around the perimeter of the plate.

In a bowl toss the peppers, celery, carrots, and fruit. Mix well and place in the center of the plate forming a mound. Remove the grilled chicken from the heat, and cut into 1/4" slices and place on top of the veg/fruit mixture. Drizzle the dressing over the salad and sprinkle with sesame seeds.

Approximate Cooking Time: 6-8 minutes

Sesame Dressing (1 cup)

2 ounces	Granulated Sugar
1 tsp.	Dry Mustard
2 TB.	Soy Sauce
1/2 cup	Salad Oil
1/2 cup	Sesame Oil
3 TB.	White Vinegar

Place the sugar, mustard and soy sauce in a bowl and combine until sugar is dissolved. Slowly whip in the oil and vinegar in alternating fashion. Continue to whip until the dressing emulsifies.

Grilled Salads

Grilled Shrimp Nicoise Salad

2 entree salads

Ingredients:

4 each	Leaf Lettuce, leaves
2 cups	Red Potatoes, sliced grilled, marinade in Italian dressing
1 cup	Artichoke Hearts, jarred, marinated.
1/2 cup	Grilled Yellow Peppers, cut into 1" cubes
1/2 cup	Grilled Red Peppers, cut into 1" cubes
12 each	Mustard Grilled Shrimp, (p. 139)
4 each	Tomato Wedges
12 each	Whole Black Olives, pitted

Heat Source:
Direct fire, high heat (reference pg. 7-10)

Preparation:
Heat grill to high heat. Lightly oil the grates before grilling the shrimp and vegetables.

Slice and grill the red potatoes, before marinating in the Italian dressing. Grill the peppers, this can be done whole and then cubed or cubed and placed on skewers for ease of grilling.

Place half the lettuce leaves on a 10" round plate, covering the plate in the center. Mound the grilled peppers in the center of the plate. Place the grilled shrimp on top of the peppers. Divide the potatoes, artichoke hearts, tomatoes and olives in two and place around the outer perimeter of the salad.

Serve warm.

Approximate Cooking Time: 6-8 minutes

Special Note:
Make sure all your vegetable prep and shrimp prep is done, before starting, you want to serve this salad warm.

If you like extra dressing, use your favorite Italian dressing splash with a hint of stone ground mustard for an added zest to the salad!

Oranges with Grilled Fennel & Red Onion

4 side salads

Ingredients:

4 each	*Oranges, peeled and sliced*
1 small	*Fennel Bulb, cored, quartered*
1 small	*Red onion, peeled, quartered*
4 TB.	*Balsamic Vinegar*
1 TB.	*Brown Sugar*
as needed	*Fresh Fennel Leaves, minced*

Heat Source:
Direct fire, medium heat (reference pg. 7-10)

Preparation:
Heat grill to medium heat. Lightly oil the grates before grilling the vegetables.

Prepare the fennel bulb and red onion. Grill the quartered pieces until just tender. Remove from the grill and slice the fennel and red onion into thin slices. Place in a bowl and toss with the vinegar and brown sugar. Cover with saran wrap and allow to sit for about 30 minutes.

With a sharp small knife, cut away the outer peel and membrane of the orange, leaving the whole orange intact. Slice each orange into 4-5 crosscut slices and place one sliced orange on each salad plate. This can be done ahead and allowed to sit at room temperature, which will bring out the flavor of the orange.

After the marinated fennel and red onion have set for 30 minutes. Top the orange slices with the fennel/onion mix. Pour the remaining vinegar mixture over the salads and top with the fresh chopped fennel leaves.

Approximate Cooking Time: 6 minutes

Grilled Asparagus Salad with Red Pepper Mayonnaise

4 side salads

Ingredients:

2 pounds	Fresh Asparagus, cleaned
1/2 cup	Balsamic Vinegar
2 TB.	Brown Sugar
1 each	Red Pepper, whole
1/2 cup	Mayonnaise
2 TB.	Lemon Juice, fresh
to taste	Salt
to taste	White Pepper
1 TB.	Parsley, fresh, chopped

Heat Source:
Direct fire, medium heat (reference pg. 7-10)

Preparation:
Heat grill to medium heat. Lightly oil the grates before grilling the vegetables.

Clean and wash the asparagus, dry well. Place in a shallow dish and sprinkle the top of the asparagus with the brown sugar. drizzle the asparagus with the balsamic vinegar. Allow to sit for 30-45 minutes.

Wash and seed the red pepper, lightly oil the red pepper and grill on all sides until charred and soft. Remove the pepper and allow to cool. Once cooled peel away the outer membrane of the pepper, cut in half and remove the seeds. Puree the pepper using a cuisinart. Once the pepper is a smooth puree, add the mayonnaise and lemon juice to form a smooth sauce. Season to taste.

After the asparagus has marinated, removed from the vinegar/sugar mixture and place on the grill. Grill the asparagus until cooked and tender. Turning several times. Place the warm grilled asparagus on a salad plate and drizzle the red pepper mayonnaise over the asparagus.

Garnish with chopped parsley and serve.

Approximate Cooking Time: 5-6 minutes

Taste Bud Marinades

Marinades

Margarita Marinade for Chicken

1 cup

Ingredients:

1/4 cup	*Tequila*
1/4 cup	*Lime Juice, fresh*
1/4 cup	*Triple Sec*
1/4 cup	*Honey*

Preparation:

Mix all the ingredients together and blend well.

Enough for marinating 4 - 6 ounces boneless chicken breast.

Lamb Marinade

enough for 5 Pounds of lamb

Ingredients:

1 quart	*Olive Oil*
3 TB.	*Rosemary, fresh*
1 1/2 TB.	*Oregano, dried*
1 TB.	*Black Pepper, coarse ground*
1 pint	*Lemon Juice, fresh*
1 pint	*Vermouth, dry*
1/4 cup	*Garlic, fine minced*
1 1/2 cups	*Mint Leaves, fresh, chopped*

Preparation:

Combine all the ingredients and blend well. Hold at room temperature for use in marinating and basting of lamb.

Notes: Enough for one 5 pound leg of lamb.

Tuscan Marinade

1 1/2 quarts

Ingredients:

3 cups	*Olive Oil*
3/4 cup	*Balsamic Vinegar*
2 TB.	*Rosemary, fresh*
1 TB.	*Oregano, dried*
1 TB.	*Black Pepper, coarse ground*
1 cup	*Basil, fresh, chopped*
1 cup	*Parsley, chopped*
4 ounces	*Garlic, fine minced*

Preparation:

Mix all the ingredients together and blend well. Make fresh as needed for each recipe.

London Broil Marinade

enough for 3 Pounds of Flank steak

Ingredients:

3 cups	*Water, cold*
1 cups	*Burgundy Wine*
2 TB.	*Red Wine Vinegar*
1/2 cup	*White Onions, sliced thin*
1 each	*Garlic Cloves, crushed*
1 tsp.	*Thyme Leaves, dry*
1 tsp.	*Oregano, ground*
1 tsp.	*Black Pepper, ground*
1 tsp.	*Salt Table*

Preparation:
Combine liquids to blend completely. Add the onions, garlic, herbs and seasonings to the marinade and stir to mix.

Special Note:
Marinade can be used 2 times before discarding.

All Purpose Marinade
enough for 4 pounds of product

Ingredients:

2 cups	Salad Oil
1 cup	Dry Vermouth
1/4 cup	Lemon Juice, fresh
3 TB.	Lemon Pepper
1 TB.	Cracked Black Pepper
1 TB.	Kosher Salt
1 TB.	Fresh Garlic, minced
1/2 cup	Fresh Flat Parsley, minced

Preparation:
Combine all the ingredients together and blend well. Hold cold for use.

Special Note:
Let marinade come to room temperature before using. Stir marinade to incorporate the ingredients again, before using.

This makes a great All Purpose marinade for poultry & pork!

Use 1 cup of marinade per 2 pounds of meat.

Mustard Marinade for Shrimp

2 cups

Ingredients:

1 1/2 cups	*Salad Oil*
1/2 cup	*Dry White Wine*
1 TB.	*Lemon Juice, fresh*
3 TB.	*Stone Ground Dijon Mustard*
1 tsp.	*Cracked Black Pepper*
1 tsp.	*Kosher Salt*
1 tsp.	*Fresh Dill, minced*

Preparation:

Combine all the ingredients together and blend well. Hold cold for use.

Special Note:

Let marinade come to room temperature before using. Stir marinade to incorporate the ingredients again, before using.

1 cup of marinade is needed per pound on shrimp

Orange Soy Hoisin Marinade

1 1/2 cups

Ingredients:

1/2 cup	Soy Sauce
1/2 cup	Orange Juice, fresh
4 TB.	Rice Wine Vinegar
2 TB.	Sesame Oil
2 TB.	Garlic, fresh, minced
1 TB.	Hoisin Sauce
1 TB.	Brown Sugar
1/2 tsp.	Ginger, ground

Preparation:
Combine all ingredients and blend well.

Special Notes: Use with pork tender or pork loin. Place meat in a container and pour the marinade over the pork, marinade for at least 12 hours or overnight.

Enough for 2 pounds of meat.

Fajita Marinade

1 quart

Ingredients:

3/4 cup	Lime Juice, fresh
3/4 cup	Water, cold
1 cup	Soy Sauce
1 cup	Teriyaki Marinade, "Kikkoman's"®
3/4 cup	Dark Brown Sugar
1/3 cup	Molasses
1 tsp. tsp.	Ginger, ground

Preparation:

Combine all ingredients in a large sauce pan. Bring to a full boil. Remove from heat, cool down, and refrigerate until needed.

Special Notes: Use with beef or chicken. Place meat in a container and pour the marinade over the beef or chicken, marinate for at least 4 hours.

Enough for 2 pounds of meat.

Coconut Curry Marinade

enough for one pound of scallops

Ingredients:

2 TB.	*Peanut Oil*
1 cup	*Coconut Milk, canned*
4 TB.	*Brown Sugar*
2 cloves	*Garlic, minced*
2 tsp.	*Curry Powder*

Preparation:

Combine all ingredients and pour marinade over the scallops and marinate for 2 hours under refrigeration.

Unconfused
Infused Oils

Sage, Garlic & Peppercorn Oil

Makes 1 cup

Ingredients:

1 cup	*Olive Oil*
1/4 cup	*Sage, fresh, rough chopped*
1/2 cup	*Garlic, fresh, minced*
2 tsp.	*Cracked Black Pepper*

Preparation:
Heat the oil in a small pan on the grill over medium heat. Once the oil is warm not hot add the remaining ingredients. Let warm olive oil set at room temperature for one hour, to infuse the flavors.

Special Note:
This oil is very good for dipping chicken breast, lamb chops or pork chops in before grilling. Use the infused oil for oiling the grates before grilling also.

Rosemary & Pepper Oil

Makes 1 cup

Ingredients:

1 cup	*Olive Oil*
1/4 cup	*Rosemary, fresh, rough chopped*
2 tsp.	*Cracked Black Pepper*

Preparation:

Heat the oil in a small pan on the grill over medium heat. Once the oil is warm not hot add the remaining ingredients. Let warm olive oil set at room temperature for one hour, to infuse the flavors.

Special Note:

This oil is very good for dipping lamb or swordfish steaks in before grilling. Use the infused oil for oiling the grates before grilling also.

Roasted Red Pepper Oil

Makes 1 cup

Ingredients:

1 cup	*Olive Oil*
1/4 cup	*Roasted Red Peppers, charred, puree*
1/2 cup	*Garlic, fresh, minced*
1 tsp.	*Red Pepper Flakes, crushed*

Preparation:
Char the red peppers whole on the grill before adding to the oil. Once charred, remove the outer skin when cooled and remove the inner seeds. Puree the peppers in a cuisinart.

Heat the oil in a small pan on the grill over medium heat. Once the oil is warm not hot add the remaining ingredients. Let warm olive oil set at room temperature for one hour, to infuse the flavors.

Special Note:
This oil is very good for chicken, medium flavored fish for grilling, (salmon and sword). And is excellent for grilling scallops and shrimp.

Sundried Tomato & Basil Oil

Makes 1 cup

Ingredients:

1 cup	*Olive Oil*
1/4 cup	*Sundried Tomatoes, packed in oil, drained and minced finely*
1/2 cup	*Garlic, fresh, minced*
1 TB.	*Basil, fresh, minced*

Preparation:
Heat the oil in a small pan on the grill over medium heat. Once the oil is warm not hot add the remaining ingredients. Let warm olive oil set at room temperature for one hour, to infuse the flavors.

Special Note:
This oil is very good for chicken, shrimp and scallops.

New World of Grilled & Seared Meats

Tuscan Grilled Steaks

4 steaks

Ingredients:

4 each	*Strip Steaks, trimmed of outer fat*
1 quart	*Tuscan Marinade (p. 93)*

Heat Source:
Direct fire, high heat (reference pg. 7-10)

Preparation:
Trim the steaks of any outer fat. It is not needed when using this marinade. Place the steaks in a shallow pan and pour the marinade over the steaks, turn the steaks to make sure that the meat is coated well on both sides. Allow the meat to sit at room temperature for about 1 hour.

Pre heat the grill with high heat. Once the grill is hot, oil lightly with some olive oil.

Drain the steaks from any excess marinade and place on the grill. Grill on both sides for about 5-6 minutes for 1" thick steaks to achieve a medium rare cooked steak.

Remove the steaks from the grill and serve.

Special Note:
When using marinades made with oil, you may get some flare up from the oil dripping on the burners or coal. Use a spray bottle with water to put out the flare ups. Also have one grill area set to low heat for moving the meat while controlling flare ups.

Steak Au Poivre

4 steaks

Ingredients:
4 each	*Strip Steaks, trimmed of outer fat*
4 TB.	*Cracked Black Pepper*
1 cup	*Cracked Pepper Sauce*

Heat Source:
Direct fire, high heat (reference pg. 7-10)

Preparation:
Trim the steaks of any outer fat. Place the steaks on a cutting board and coat each side with the cracked pepper. Using 1 tablespoon per steak. Press the pepper into the meat slightly. Allow the steaks to sit at room temperature for 1 hour before grilling.

Pre heat the grill with high heat. Once the grill is hot, oil lightly with some olive oil.

Sear the steaks over the high heat side on each side for 4-5 minutes for a 1" thick steak for medium rare doneness. The high heat with bring out the sweetness in the cracked pepper. Remove the steaks from the grill. Place on warm plate and place 2 oz. of Cracked Pepper Sauce over half the steak.

Cracked Pepper Sauce:(1 cup)
1 ounce	*Melted Butter*
3 TB.	*Shallots, minced*
2 TB.	*Brandy*
1 tsp.	*Cracked Black Pepper*
1 cup	*Beef Broth, canned*
1/2 cup	*Heavy Cream*

In a sauce pan on the grill, add the butter and shallots and cook until shallots turn golden brown. Add the cracked pepper and brandy. Allow the brandy to reduce down almost dry. Add the beef broth and bring to a boil. Add the cream and bring to a boil again. Allow the sauce to simmer until reduced to about 1 cup of sauce. This should thicken the sauce slightly. Hold warm until steaks are cooked. Ladle over half the cooked steak and serve.

World's Best Burgers

8-10 burgers

Ingredients:

3 pounds	*Ground Chuck, 80/20*
1 TB.	*Lemon Pepper*
1 TB.	*Seasoning Salt*
1 TB.	*Rub Me Tender Dry Rub (p. 168)*
1/4 cup	*A-1® Steak Sauce*
1/4 cup	*BBQ Sauce, book recipe or favorite*

Heat Source:
Direct fire, high heat (reference pg. 7-10)

Preparation:
Combine the ground chuck with all the dry and liquid ingredients. Mix to blend well. Form into 6" burgers, 1" thick, grill over hot fire until desired temperature.

Use one of Rib Stars BBQ Sauces or use your favorite, you can't go wrong with these burgers!

Approximate Cooking Time: Allow 5-6 minutes per side for medium doneness.

Grilled & Seared Meats

Hawg's Breath Pork Ribs

3 slabs

Ingredients:

3 Slabs	*Baby Back Ribs, peeled*
6 TB.	*Hawg's Breath Rib Rub (p. 169)*
1 cup	*Hawg's Breath Rib Mop, room temp.*
3/4 cup	*Hawg's Breath BBQ Sauce, (p. 164), room temp.*

Heat Source:

Direct fire, medium heat (reference pg. 7-10)
Indirect fire, medium heat (reference pg. 7-10)

Preparation:

Remove the membrane from the back of the ribs. Paint each slab of ribs with the Mop and marinade for 2 hours.

Sprinkle each side of the ribs with the rib rub and place the ribs on the side of the grill over direct heat. Grill the ribs on both sides for about 15 minutes, turning several times to keep the ribs from burning. Once the ribs have browned nicely, move to the side of the grill with no heat, keep the indirect fire at a medium heat. Close the lid of the grill and grill roast the ribs for 4-5 hours or until tender. Meat will pull away from the bone when done. Maintain the inside temperature of the grill at 300° F while cooking ribs.

Mop ribs about every hour with the Rib Mop. 30 minutes before serving ribs, brush both sides of the ribs with the Hawg's Breath BBQ Sauce. Ribs can be placed back over the direct fire, just before serving to glaze the sauce.

Special Note:

When moving ribs to indirect side, you can place a wood box or wood chucks over your direct fire side to give the ribs some nice smoked flavor on the outside of the ribs.

Hawg's Breath Rib Mop (3 cups)

2 cups	*Pineapple or Apple Juice*
1/4 cup	*Maple Syrup, real*
1/4 cup	*White Vinegar*
1/4 cup	*Pick A Pepper Sauce®*
1/4 cup	*Worcestershire Sauce*

Combine all ingredients together and place on the heat. Bring to a boil and remove from the heat, hold warm for service.

Grilled Lamb Chops

4 portions

Ingredients:

8 each	*Lamb Chops, double bone , frenched*
1/2 recipe	*Lamb Marinade, (p.92)*

Heat Source:
Direct fire, medium heat (reference pg. 7-10)

Preparation:
Place the lamb chops in a shallow pan and pour the lamb marinade over the chops. Turn the chops and make sure that they are coated well on both side with the marinade. Marinate the lamb for at least 12 hours or over night.

Preheat the grill on medium heat. While the grill is preheating, remove the chops from the marinade and allow to sit at room temperature until the grill is ready. Once the grill is ready, oil the grates lightly and place the chops on the grill. Once the chops are cooked, remove them from the grill and serve.

Approximate Cooking Time: 5-6 minutes on each side for 1" chops for medium rare doneness

Special Note:
If the bones tend to burn, cover them with aluminum foil before grilling. Remove the foil before serving the chops.

Beef Fajitas

4 portions

Ingredients:

1 1/2 pounds	*Beef Flank*
1 TB.	*Lemon Pepper*
1 cup	*Fajita Marinade (p.98)*
8 ea.	*8" Flour Tortillas, warm*
4 oz.	*Red & Yellow Peppers, cleaned, seeded, cut in strips.*
4 oz.	*Green Peppers, cleaned, seeded, cut in strips.*
8 oz.	*White Onion, peeled, cut in half and thinly sliced.*
1 each	*Lime, fresh, cut in half*

Heat Source:
Direct fire, medium heat (reference pg. 7-10)

Preparation:
Trim flank steak of any excess fat. Season the beef with lemon pepper and place in a clean container. Pour the fajita marinade over the meat and marinade for at least 6 hours.

Prepare the peppers and onions and grill using a grill grid or pan. Cook until al dente (halfway). Set aside and hold warm.

Turn grill on and while grill is heating, remove the meat from the marinade. Place the meat on the grill. Grill on both sides of the meat until the meat is cooked to desired temperature. Slice the meat across the grain about 1/4" thick. While the meat is grilling, heat a cast iron fillet skillet on the grill on medium heat.

Place the cooked cooked peppers and onions on the hot skillet, lay the sliced beef fajita meat on top of the peppers and onion mixture. Squeeze the fresh lime juice over the meat and serve immediately with the flour tortillas.

Approximate Cooking Time: 10-12 minutes

Special Note:
Traditional garnishes are: diced tomatoes, shredded lettuce, grated cheese, sour cream, salsa and guacamole.

Blackened Filet Medallions

4 portions

Ingredients:

8 each	4 oz. Filet Medallions
8 TB.	Blackened Seasoning
2 TB.	Olive Oil or Grape Seed Oil
4 cups	Warm Jalapeno Corn Relish (p. 192)

Heat Source:
Direct fire, high heat (reference pg. 7-10)

Preparation:
Prepare the seasoning mix. Season the medallions with the seasoning on both sides, using about 1 tablespoon per steak. Press the seasoning into the meat lightly. Allow the meat to sit at room temperature while grill is preheating.

Using the flat griddle of your gas grill, preheat it on high heat. If using a coal grill, use a flat cast iron skillet and heat it directly over the coals.

Once the griddle is hot, lightly coat with the oil, not much oil is needed, just enough to keep the seasoned steaks from sticking and burning.

Place the seasoned filets on the oiled griddle and sear on both sides for 2-3 minutes per side (1/2" thick) for medium rare. While filets are cooking warm the relish on the grill in a small pan. Place about a 1/2 cup of relish on the plate and place the cooked filets on top of the corn relish.

Blackened Seasoning (1 cup)

2 TB.	Salt
2 tsp.	Cayenne Pepper
2 tsp.	Black Pepper
2 tsp.	Oregano Leaves, dry
2 tsp.	Basil Leaves, dry
2 tsp.	Thyme Leaves, dry
3/4 cup	Paprika
2 TB.	Garlic Powder

Combine all ingredients in a covered container and shake well to blend. Hold for preparation.

Grilled & Seared Meats

Spiced Roasted Whole Tenderloin

1 each - 5 pound Whole Tenderloin

Ingredients:

5 pound	*Beef Tenderloin, whole, trimmed fully*
1/4 cup	*Olive Oil*
2 TB.	*Garlic Salt*
2 TB.	*Onion Salt*
2 TB.	*Black Pepper, table grind*
1 TB.	*Chili Powder*
1 tsp.	*Cayenne Pepper*
1 tsp.	*Cumin, ground*

Heat Source:

Direct fire, high heat (reference pg. 7-10)
Indirect fire, medium heat (reference pg. 7-10)

Preparation:

Using a clean, dry cutting board, trim the tenderloin of all fat and silver skin tissue and remove the side strap. After trimming the tenderloin, cut-off 3" from the flat tail end, reserving the tail meat for other uses like grilling beef kabobs.

Preheat the grill, if searing on a gas grill and if you have a griddle top, lightly oil the griddle top and sear the tenderloin on this part of the grill. If you do not have a griddle top, then sear the tenderloin on the grates of the grill over a high heat fire.

After oiling the tenderloin, mix the spices together and uniformly sprinkle seasoning over the meat. Carefully rub the seasoning into the flesh of the meat insuring a uniform distribution. Immediately sear the whole tenderloin on the grill, turning often to thoroughly char brown all sides and ends of the roast. When the tenderloin is well browned, remove it from the searing high heat grill and move it to the off side of the grill, turn the indirect heat down to low and close the lid. Roast the tenderloin until done, about 30 minutes. Internal temperature should be 145° F,

Remove from the grill and allow to sit for 15 minutes covered, before slicing.

Special Note:

You can also just buy a fully trimmed tenderloin from your butcher.

Kifta

(Mediterranean Spiced Grilled Skewered Ground Meat)
2 pounds of mixture - 16 kiftas
4 orders

Ingredients:

2 pound	Ground Beef (75/25 mixture)
1/2 cup	Parsley, fresh, chopped
1/2 cup	White Onion, finely minced
2 tsp.	Kosher Salt
2 tsp.	Black Pepper, table grind
1 tsp.	Cinnamon, ground
1 tsp.	All Spice, ground
3 TB.	Ice Cold Water
4 ea.	Pita Bread, warmed on the grill
1 cup	Romaine, finely shredded
1 ea.	Tomatoe, cut in half, sliced thin
1/2 cup	Red Onion, sliced thin
1 cup	Cucumbers, sliced thin
1/4	Yogurt
1 tsp.	Mint, fresh, minced

Heat Source:
Direct fire, medium heat (reference pg. 7-10)

Preparation:
Place the ground beef and other ingredients except water in very cold stainless steel bowl. While mixing ingredients together, add ice water in two parts, to keep the meat cold and moist. Moisten your hands with ice water while forming meat. Mix meat until mixture tightens. Form into 2 oz. cylinder shape and skewer using a bamboo skewer. Place two kiftas on each skewer

Preheat the grill, lightly oil the grill before grilling kifta. Grill kifta on all sides until done, about 6-8 minutes. Once grilled remove from the fire and serve with warm cut pita bread, shredded romaine leaves, thin sliced tomatoes, thin sliced red onions and sliced cucumbers (tossed in yogurt with fresh minced mint).

Approximate Cooking Time: 5-6 minutes

Special Note:
This special recipe was taught to me by Peggy Haddad.

Grilled & Seared Meats

London Broil

3 pound flank steak
4-6 portions

Ingredients:

1 each	*3# Flank steak, trimmed*
1 quart	*London Broil Marinade (p. 94), cold*

Heat Source:
Direct fire, medium heat (reference pg. 7-10)

Preparation:
Score the London broil (flank steak) across the meat diagonally with a sharp knife, on both sides no deeper than 1/8". Place the meat into the marinade and marinate for 24 hours under refrigeration.

While grill is heating up, drain the flank steak and pat dry. Oil the grates of the grill before placing the flank steak onto the grill.

Once the flank is done, allow it to rest for 15-20 minutes before slicing. Slice on a bias in thin long slices across the grain of the meat.

Approximate Cooking Time: 15-20 minutes

Special Note:
Cook London Broil until medium rare. The cooking time will depend on the thickness of the flank steak. 1" thick flank steak will take about 15 -20 minutes total cooking time.

Seared Veal Scaloppini

4 portions

Ingredients:

8 each	2 oz. Veal Scaloppini, thin and flattened
1 cup	Flour
as needed	Salt
as needed	White Pepper
3 TB.	Olive Oil or Grape Seed Oil
8 TB.	Lemon Caper Herb Butter, soft

Heat Source:
Direct fire, high heat (reference pg. 7-10)

Preparation:
Prepare the seasoning flour, by mixing in the salt and pepper well. Dredge the flattened veal into the flour and shake of any excess flour.

Using the flat griddle of your gas grill, preheat it on high heat. If using a coal grill, use a flat cast iron skillet and heat it directly over the coals.

Once the griddle is hot, coat with the oil, not much oil is needed, just enough to keep the floured scaloppini from sticking and burning.

Place the floured scaloppini on the oiled griddle and sear on both sides for 2-3 minutes per side (1/4" thick) for medium. Once seared and golden brown on both sides, remove from the grill and place on a warm serving platter and top with the softened Lemon Caper Herb Butter.

Special Note:
If needed, because of the flour you may need to add oil as they are cooking, to ensure that the scaloppini do not stick.

Lemon Caper Herb Butter (1/2 cup)

1/2 cup	Sweet Butter, unsalted, soft
1 each	Juice of Lemon
1 TB.	Capers, minced
1 TB.	Italian Parsley, fresh, minced
1 tsp.	Hot Sauce

Combine the softened butter with the remaining ingredients and mix well. Hold butter soft for topping the veal, this allows to butter to melt by the warmth of the meat.

Grilled & Seared Meats

Grilled Orange Soy Hoisin Pork Loin

4-6 portions

Ingredients:

2 pounds	Pork Loin, boneless
1/2 cup	Soy Sauce
1/2 cup	Orange Juice, fresh
4 TB.	Rice Wine Vinegar
2 TB.	Sesame Oil
1 TB.	Hoisin Sauce
2 TB.	Garlic, fresh minced
1 TB.	Brown Sugar
1 tsp.	Ginger, ground

Heat Source:
Direct fire, medium heat then low heat (reference pg. 7-10)

Preparation:
Combine all the ingredients together and blend well. Place meat in a container and pour the marinade over the pork, marinate for at least 4 hours or overnight.

While grill is heating up, drain the pork loin and pat dry. Oil the grates of the grill before placing the loin onto the grill.

Sear the loin on all sides and then turn the heat to low and roast with lid close until pork loin is done. 155° F internal temperature.

Once cooked remove the pork loin from the grill and allow to sit for 10 minutes before slicing.

Approximate Cooking Time: 15-20 minutes

Special Note:
Can also be used on pork tenderloins

Teriyaki Ribeye Steaks

4 portions

Ingredients:

3/4 cup	Tomato Puree, canned
1/4 cup	Pineapple Juice, canned
1/4 cup	Soy Sauce, low sodium
1/3 cup	Rice Wine Vinegar
1/2 tsp.	Ginger, ground
3 TB.	Molasses, unsulphured
1 tsp.	Caramel Color
2 TB.	Brown Sugar, dark brown
1 tsp.	Garlic Powder
4 each	Ribeye Steaks, trimmed, 1" inch, 8 oz each

Heat Source:
Direct fire, medium heat (reference pg. 7-10)

Preparation:
Place all ingredient, except the steaks in a large sauce pot. Stir with a whip to blend ingredients thoroughly, then place on the stove and bring to a full boil. As soon as the sauce boils, allow to simmer ONE MINUTE ONLY, then cool the sauce completely before using to marinade meat.

Place meat in a container and pour the Teriyaki Marinade over the steaks and marinate for at least 4 hours.

While grill is heating up, drained the steaks. Oil the grates of the grill before placing the steaks onto the grill.

Approximate Cooking Time: 4-5 minutes per side for medium rare.

Special Note:
Be careful of using a direct fire, high heat with these steaks, since the BBQ style teriyaki marinade will burn if it is cooked on a hot fire.

Grilled & Seared Meats

Plump & Juicy Poultry

Chicken Fajitas

4 portions

Ingredients:

4 ea.	Chicken Breast, boneless, skinless, 6 oz
1 TB.	Lemon Pepper
1 cup	Fajita Marinade (p.98)
8 ea.	8" Flour Tortillas, warm
4 oz.	Red & Yellow Peppers, cleaned, seeded, cut in strips.
4 oz.	Green Peppers, cleaned, seeded, cut in strips.
8 oz.	White Onion, peeled, cut in half and thinly sliced.
1 each	Lime, fresh, cut in half

Heat Source:
Direct fire, medium heat (reference pg. 7-10)

Preparation:
Trim the chicken of any excess fat. Season the the chicken with lemon pepper and place in a clean container. Pour the fajita marinade over the breast and marinade for at least 12 hours.

Prepare the peppers and onions and grill using a grill grid or pan. Cook until al dente (halfway). Set aside and hold warm.

Turn grill on and while grill is heating, remove the chicken from the marinade. When ready to grill place the chicken on the grill well on both sides of the meat. While the meat is grilling, heat a cast iron flat fajita skillet on the grill on medium heat. Once the chicken is cooked, sliced the breast across the grain about 1/4" thick.

Place the cooked peppers and onions on the hot fajita skillet, lay the sliced fajita chicken on top of the peppers and onion mixture. Squeeze the fresh lime juice over the meat and serve immediately with the flour tortillas.

Approximate Cooking Time: 10-12 minutes

Special Note:
Traditional garnishes are: diced tomatoes, shredded lettuce, grated cheese, sour cream, salsa and guacamole.

Plump & Juicy Poultry

Herb Grilled Double Breast of Chicken

4 portions

Ingredients:

4 each	Double Breast, bone in, skin-on, 10-12 oz. each
3 cups	All Purpose Marinade (p. 95)
4 TB.	Lemon Sage Butter

Heat Source:
Direct fire, medium heat then low heat (reference pg. 7-10)

Preparation:
Remove the middle kiel bone from the breast. Wash the chicken well in cold water. Pat dry. Place the breast in a shallow pan and pour the all purpose marinade over the chicken, coating both sides.

Marinate the chicken for 4 to 5 hours.

While grill is heating up, drain the chicken from any excess marinade. Oil the grates of the grill before placing the breast onto the grill.

Grill the chicken over medium heat with the skin side down too make nice crisscross grill marks on the breast. Turn the chicken over onto the bone side and turn the heat down to low. Shut the lid and roast the breast until 165° F internal temperature.

Approximate Cooking Time: 15 minutes

Lemon Sage Butter (1/2 cup)

8 ounces	Butter, unsalted, softened
1 TB.	Sage, fresh, minced
1 each	Lemon, juice and zest, chopped
1 tsp.	Lemon Pepper

Combine all the ingredients together and mix well. Hold softened for service. Topped the grilled chicken breast with 1 tablespoon of the Lemon Sage Butter.

Rub Me Tender Chicken

1 each 2 1/2 pound chicken

Ingredients:

1 each	*Whole chicken 2 1/2 pounds, cut into 8 pieces*
1 quart	*WishBone® Italian Dressing*
as needed	*Rib Stars™ Rub Me Tender BBQ Rub (p. 168)*
as needed	*Rib Stars™ Double "J" BBQ Sauce (p. 163)*

Heat Source:
Direct fire, medium heat then low heat (reference pg. 7-10)

Preparation:
Cut the whole chicken into 8 pieces (2 breast, 2 thighs, 2 legs & 2 wings). Wash the pieces of chicken in cold water with a squeeze of lemon juice. Place the cut chicken in a deep bowl and pour the dressing over the chicken and toss well to evenly coat all the pieces. Allow the chicken to marinate for 12 hours.

While grill is heating up, drained the chicken from any excess dressing and lightly season with the rub on both sides. Do not over seasoning the chicken, since chicken is easy to over power with rubs. Oil the grates of the grill before placing the chicken onto the grill.

Grill the chicken over medium heat with the skin side down too make nice grill marks on the chicken. Turn the chicken over onto the bone side and turn the heat down to low. After slow grilling the chicken, about 10 minutes, before the chicken is done, brush the skin side of the chicken with the the RibStars BBQ Sauce and slow grill with lid shut for 5 minutes. Turn the chicken back on the skin side and brush the bone side with more sauce, slow grill with lid shut for 5 minutes and then turn the chicken over to the skin side again and grill 10 minutes longer or until 165° F internal temperature. Remove and serve.

Approximate Cooking Time: 15-20 minutes

Special Note:
If you like more sauce on your chicken you can brush the chicken a second time after turning.

Scaloppini of Chicken

4 portions

Ingredients:

4 each	*6 ounce Chicken Breast, skinless*
1 cup	*All Purpose Marinade (p. 95)*
as needed	*Lemon Pepper*
as needed	*Lemon Herb Butter*

Heat Source:
Direct fire, medium heat (reference pg. 7-10)

Preparation:
Place the skinned chicken breast on a cutting board and cover with saran wrap. Pound the breast lightly until it is only about 1/4" thick and even from edge to edge. Place the flattened breast in a shallow pan and pour the marinade over the breast, coating both sides. Marinate the breast for about 2 hours.

While grill is heating up, drain the chicken from any excess marinade and lightly season with the lemon pepper on both sides. Oil the grates of the grill before placing the chicken onto the grill.

Grill the chicken on both sides over medium heat too make nice grill marks on the breast. Chicken will cook fast because it is flattened, 2-3 minutes on each side.

Approximate Cooking Time: 4-6 minutes

Lemon Herb Butter (1/2 cup)

1/2 cup	*Sweet Butter, unsalted, soft*
1 each	*Juice of Lemon*
1 TB.	*Fresh Thyme, minced*
1 TB.	*Fresh Oregano, minced*
1 TB.	*Italian Parsley, fresh, minced*

Combine the softened butter with the remaining ingredients and mix well. Hold butter soft for topping the breast, this allows the butter to melt by the warmth of the meat.

Margarita Chicken

4 portions

Ingredients:

4 each	*Chicken Breast, 6 ounce, skinless, boneless*
to taste	*Kosher Salt*
to taste	*Black Pepper*
1 recipe	*Margarita Marinade (p. 91)*

Heat Source:
Direct fire, medium heat (reference pg. 7-10)

Preparation:
Season the chicken with a 50/50 mixture of Kosher Salt and Black Pepper. Pour the marinade over the chicken and allow to marinate for 2-3 hours before grilling.

Preheat the grill with medium heat. Lightly oil the grill before placing the chicken breast on the grill.

Remove the chicken from the marinade, and place on the grill. Grill on both sides until the chicken is done. 3-4 minutes per side.

Approximate Cooking Time: 6-8 minutes

Special Note:
Extra marinade can be made to baste the chicken while cooking if desired.

Grill Roasted Chicken Thighs

2 pounds

Ingredients:

8-10 each	*Chicken Thighs, bone in*
1 quart	*Apple Cider*
1/4 cup	*Honey*
as needed	*Hawg's Breath Rib Rub (p. 169)*
as needed	*Hawg's Breath BBQ Sauce (p. 164)*

Heat Source:
Direct fire, medium heat then low heat (reference pg. 7-10)

Preparation:
Trim the thighs of any excess fat. Wash the pieces of chicken in cold water with a squeeze of lemon juice. Place the cut chicken in a deep bowl and pour the apple cider and honey over the chicken and toss well to evenly coat all the pieces. Allow the chicken to marinade for 12 hours.

While grill is heating up, drain the chicken from the cider, pat dry and lightly season with the rub on both sides. Do not over seasoning the chicken, since chicken is easy to over power with rubs. Oil the grates of the grill before placing the chicken onto the grill.

Grill the thighs over medium heat with the skin side down too make nice grill marks on the chicken. Turn the chicken over onto the bone side and turn the heat down to low. After slow grilling the chicken, about 10 minutes, before the chicken is done, brush the skin side of the meat with the the Hawg's Breath BBQ Sauce and slow grill with lid shut for 5 minutes. Turn the chicken back on the skin side and brush the bone side with more sauce, slow grill with lid shut for 5 minutes and then turn the chicken over to the skin side again and grill 10 minutes longer or until 165° F internal temperature. Remove and serve.

Approximate Cooking Time: 15-20 minutes

Shish Taouk

(Marinated Chicken Skewers)
4 portions

Ingredients:

2 pounds	Chicken Thigh Meat, boned
8 each	Whole Button Mushrooms, washed
8 each	Cocktail Onions, jarred
1 cup	Olive Oil
1/4 cup	White Wine Vinegar
1/4 cup	White Wine, dry
1 TB.	Oregano Leaves, dried
1 TB.	Rosemary, chopped fine
1 TB.	Garlic, fresh, minced
2 TB.	Lemon Juice, fresh
2 tsp.	Cracked Black Pepper

Heat Source:
Direct fire, medium heat (reference pg. 7-10)

Preparation:
Cut the thigh meat into 1" cubes, wash the mushrooms and rinse the jarred cocktail onions. Using bamboo skewers place a mushroom cap on first then two pieces of chicken, and then an onion. Repeat this procedure, putting two mushroom caps, two onions and 8 ounce of chicken on each skewer (12" skewers). Kabobs can also be made smaller using 6" skewers.

Combine the oil, vinegar, wine, herbs, spices and lemon juice emulsify with a whip. Place the kabobs in a shallow pan and pour the marinade over the kabobs, coating completely. Marinate for at least 4 hours before grilling.

While grill is heating up, drain the kabobs from the marinade. Oil the grates of the grill before placing the chicken onto the grill. Grill the kabobs on all sides until done.

Approximate Cooking Time: 8-10 minutes

Plump & Juicy Poultry

Brick Grilled Chicken

4 portions

Ingredients:

4 each	Half Chickens, bone-in
3 cups	Salad Oil
1 cup	Sherry Wine Vinegar
1/2 cup	Orange Juice, concentrate
6 each	Oranges, juice and zest
6 each	Lemons, juice and zest
4 TB.	Marjoram Leaves, dried
2 TB.	Kosher Salt
2 tsp.	Lemon Pepper

Heat Source:
Direct fire, medium heat (reference pg. 7-10)
Indirect fire, medium heat (reference pg. 7-10)

Preparation:
Wash the half chickens in cold water and trim of any excess fat. Place the chicken halves in a shallow pan.

Combine the oil, vinegar, juices, zest, herbs and spices together and mix well Pour the mixture over the chicken halves and coat both sides. Make sure that the chicken stays in the marinade skin side down and marinate for 12 hours.

While grill is heating up, drain the chicken from the marinade. Oil the grates of the grill before placing the chicken onto the grill. Use a brick (cement type) wrapped well with foil, per chicken half. The bricks are used to press the chicken down while grilling, which helps flatten the chicken and makes deeper grill marks in the chicken. Place the chicken, skin side down, over the direct fire and place the wrapped bricks on top of each chicken half. Grill for 5 minutes and turn over onto the bone side, place the bricks back on top. Grill another 5 minutes and remove the bricks. Move the grilled charred chicken to the non heat side of the grill, leave the heat side on medium heat and close the lid. Roast the chicken for another 10 minutes until 165° F internal temperature.

Remove from the grill and serve.

Approximate Cooking Time: 20 minutes

Simple
Seafood

Grilled Fish Tacos

4 tacos

Ingredients:

1 pound	*Fresh Catfish Fillets, skinned, cut in strips*
1 tsp.	*Chili Powder*
1 tsp.	*Black Pepper*
1 tsp.	*Kosher Salt*
1/2 tsp.	*Cumin Powder*
4 each	*6" Soft Flour Tortillas or Fried Corn Taco Shells*
1 cup	*Shredded White Cabbage*
1/2 cup	*Diced Tomatoes*
1/2 cup	*White Onions, minced*
2 TB.	*Cilantro, minced*
2 TB.	*Jalapeno Peppers, seeded, minced*
1 ea.	*Avocado, peeled and diced*
1/2 cup	*Sour Cream*
2 TB.	*Salsa, your favorite*

Heat Source:
Direct fire, medium heat (reference pg. 7-10)

Preparation:
Combine the chili powder, pepper, salt and cumin together and mix well. Cut the catfish fillets into long strips about 1" wide, for grilling. Season the catfish fillets on both sides. Before grilling, prep all the remaining ingredients for assembling the tacos. Finely shred the cabbage, dice the tomatoes, onions, cilantro and jalapeno peppers. Combine together to make a relish. Hold for assembly of the tacos.

Combine the sour cream and the salsa together and blend well. Hold for assembly. Peel the avocados just before dicing for the tacos.

Lightly oil the grates of the grill and grill the catfish until done.

Warm the flour tortillas and lay the catfish in the center, top with the cabbage, tomato/onion mixture, avocado and salsa sour cream. Fold the taco in half and serve.

Approximate Cooking Time: 5-6 minutes

Peppered Swordfish

4 portions

Ingredients:

4 each	Fresh Swordfish Steaks, 1" thick, 8 ounce each
1 cup	Rosemary & Pepper Infused Oil (p. 104)
4 TB.	Cracked Black Pepper
1 cup	Cracked Pepper Sauce (p. 110)

Heat Source:
Direct fire, medium heat (reference pg. 7-10)

Preparation:
Prepare the infused oil and cool completely. Sprinkle the swordfish steaks on both sides with the cracked pepper. Press into the steaks lightly. Oil the grill grates with some of the infused oils.

Place the steaks into a shallow pan with the infused oil, before placing on the grill. Steaks will take about 3 to 4 minutes a side for 1" thickness. Turn 90° when grilling to achieve crisscross marks. When done remove from the grill and top half the steak with the Cracked Pepper Sauce.

Approximate Cooking Time: 8-10 minutes

Seared Ahi Tuna

4 portions

Ingredients:

4 each	*Ahi Tuna Steaks, fresh, 1" thick, 8 ounce each*
2 TB.	*White Sesame Seeds*
2 TB.	*Black Sesame Seeds (found in local oriental markets)*
4 cups	*Radish Sprout Salad*
4 ea.	*Lime Wedges*

Heat Source:
Direct fire, high heat (reference pg. 7-10)

Preparation:
Oil the grates of the grill with sesame seed oil.

Mix the two sesame seeds together and sprinkle over both sides of the tuna.

Prepare the Radish Sprout Salad ahead a couple of hours to set the flavor.

Grill the Ahi tuna over high heat. Sear the Ahi and cook to medium rare. Most high quality tuna should be eaten medium rare. to medium. Over cooking tuna will make it very dry. Cook tuna about 2 minutes a side, just putting a nice crust on each side.

Place about a cup of the radish sprout salad in the center of the plate and place the tuna steak on top of the salad. Squeeze the fresh lime juice over the top and serve.

Approximate Cooking Time: 4 minutes

Radish Sprout Salad (4 cups)

2 pint	*Radish Sprouts or Regular Sprouts*
1 each	*Cucumber, washed and cut in long thin ribbons*
1 each	*Small Red Onion, minced*
2 TB.	*Rice Wine Vinegar*
1 TB.	*Granulated Sugar*
1 each	*Juice of lime*

Combine all the ingredients together and allow the salad to sit about 4 hours before using.

Simple Seafood

Buttered Crumb Topped Scrod

4 portions

Ingredients:

4 each	*Fresh Scrod, Cod or Haddock, skin on, 8 ounce ea.*
1 cup	*Melted Butter*
as needed	*Seasoning Salt*
2 cups	*White Bread Crumbs, fresh, no crust.*

Heat Source:

Direct fire, low heat (reference pg. 7-10)
Indirect fire, high heat (reference pg. 7-10)

Preparation:

Preheat the grill, one side needs to be indirect high heat, the side of the grill with the fish on it, will be direct heat on low. The fish is grill baked.

Melt the butter and prepare the bread crumbs. Dip the fillets into the melted butter , then sprinkle lightly with seasoning salt and coat the top of the fillets with the white bread crumbs.

Place the fillets in shallow pan, add about 1/4" of water, with some of the leftover melted butter. Place the pan of fish on the low heat side and close the lid of the grill. Grill bake at 325° until fish is done and bread crumbs are browning slightly.

When the fish is done, remove the pan from the grill and lift the fillets out of the pan, carefully with a spatula and place on the plate.

Approximate Cooking Time: 15 minutes

Mustard Grilled Shrimp

4 portions

Ingredients:
2 pounds	*Raw shrimp, 16/20 ct., peeled and cleaned*
2 cup	*Mustard Marinade (p. 96)*

Heat Source:
Direct fire, medium heat (reference pg. 7-10)

Preparation:
After cleaning the shrimp, place in a glass bowl and pour the prepared marinade over the shrimp. Toss to coat well and marinate for at least 4 hours.

Preheat the grill. While grill is heating, drain the shrimp and skewer the shrimp on to 4 bamboo skewers.

Oil the grates lightly with olive oil. And lay the skewers of shrimp on the grill and cook on each side 3-4 minutes until done. Be careful not to over cook the shrimp.

Remove the shrimp from the heat and remove them from the skewer before serving.

Special Note:
Most shrimp can be bought in the stores already cleaned and peeled to save time.

Approximate Cooking Time: 6-8 minutes

Coconut Curried Scallops

2-3 portions

Ingredients:

1 pound	*Fresh Scallops,1 -2" diameter*
1 recipe	*Coconut Curry Marinade (p. 99)*

Heat Source:
Direct fire, medium heat (reference pg. 7-10)

Preparation:
Place the fresh scallops in a shallow dish for marinating. Pour the coconut curry marinade over the scallops and marinate for at least 2 hours under refrigeration.

Preheat the grill. While grill is heating, drain the scallops from the marinade. Oil the grates lightly with olive oil. And lay the scallops on the grates to sear and grill nicely. Cook the scallops about 4-5 minutes each side, being careful not to overcook them. Overcooking will make the scallop become tough.

Once grilled and seared remove from the grill and serve immediately.

Special Note:
Frozen scallops need to be thawed slowly and drained from purge before marinating.

Approximate Cooking Time: 8-10 minutes

Proscuitto Wrapped Pesto Shrimp

4 portions

Ingredients:

1 pound	*16/20 ct. Shrimp, peeled and cleaned tails on*
1 cup	*Basil Pesto (p. 67)*
4 ounces	*Proscuitto Ham, sliced paper thin*
as needed	*Fresh Grind Pepper, from pepper mill*

Heat Source:
Direct fire, medium heat (reference pg. 7-10)

Preparation:
After cleaning the shrimp, dip the shrimp in the pesto. Remove any excess pesto from the shrimp. Wrap each shrimp in the center portion of the tail with the paper thin ham, wrapping it around the shrimp completely. Place the prepared shrimp on a platter and grind some fresh pepper over the shrimp.

Preheat the grill, using medium high heat. To much heat will burn the ham before the shrimp is done. Oil the grates of the grill lightly and place the wrapped shrimp on the grates. Cook on both sides for about 3-4 minutes. Once the shrimp is cooked remove from the heat.

Special Note:
Shrimp is great served on a bed of pasta tossed with fresh diced tomatoes, olive oil, capers and Italian cured olives.

Approximate Cooking Time: 6-8 minutes

Lemon Pepper Trout

4 portions

Ingredients:

4 each	Rainbow Trout, dressed and butterflied, 8 oz. each
1 quart	Warm Water
1 cup	Brown Sugar
4 ounces	White Onion, sliced very thin
2 TB.	Kosher Salt
1 tsp.	Garlic Powder
as needed	Lemon Pepper

Heat Source:
Direct fire, medium heat (reference pg. 7-10)

Preparation:
Place the warm water in a bowl and add the sugar, onion and spices to the water. Stir to dissolve the sugar. Allow the water to cool completely. Wash the trout off and place in the brine. Brine the trout for about 4 hours. After brining, remove the trout and rinse off with cold water. Pat the trout dry and allow to air dry for 2 hours under refrigeration.

Preheat the grill, using medium heat. Lightly oil the grill. Lay the trout on a platter skin side down and sprinkle the flesh of the trout with lemon pepper. Place the trout on the hot grill, flesh side down. Cook for 2-3 minutes and turn the trout over onto the skin side and cook another 2-3 minutes until the fillet is done.

Special Note:
Trout is easier to handle as a skin on fillet.

Approximate Cooking Time: 4-6 minutes

Grilled Lobster Tail Scampi Style

4 portions

Ingredients:

4 each	Whole Lobster Tails, split and butterflied
4 TB.	Melted Butter
1 cup	Bread crumbs, fresh
2 TB.	Parsley, fresh, chopped
1 TB.	Garlic, minced fine
as needed	Seasoning Salt

Heat Source:
Direct fire, medium heat then low heat (reference pg. 7-10)

Preparation:
Rinse the lobster tails, using a sturdy chef's knife, cut the lobster shell down the back and split the tail open. DO NOT CUT ALL THE WAY THROUGH THE TAIL MEAT. Pull the tail meat out of the shell and butterfly the meat 3/4 of the way.

Hold the melted butter for grilling. Mix the fresh bread crumbs, parsley, garlic and seasoning salt together and blend well.

Preheat the grill, using medium heat. Lightly oil the grates. And place the tail on the grill, butterflied side down first. Grill about 4-5 minutes for tails weighing 6-8 ounces each. Turn the tail over, drizzle the tail with a little bit of the melted butter and top with the bread crumb mixture. Drizzle with more butter and close the lid, finish cooking the tails until done about another 5-6 minutes. When done, remove the tail from the fire. Overcooking will make the lobster tail tough.

Special Note:
Before placing the tail on the grill, turn the tail over with the butterflied side down and cut small incisions three times across the tail muscle about 1" apart. This will help the tail to grill flat while cooking, if this is not done the tail with start to curl up as it cooks.

Approximate Cooking Time: 10-15 minutes

Cooking a Clambake

4 people

Ingredients:

1 pound	*Seaweed, fresh (optional)*
8 each	*Baby Red Potatoes*
4 ears	*Corn of the cob, fresh, shucked*
4 each	*One Pound Lobsters, alive*
1 pound	*Fresh Clams, washed*
1 pound	*Fresh Mussels, cleaned & washed*
2 sprigs	*Fresh Thyme*
1 tsp.	*Freshly Ground Black Pepper*
4 cups	*White Wine Broth (p. 66)*

Heat Source:
Direct fire, high heat then medium heat (reference pg. 7-10)

Preparation:
Preheat the grill using high heat.

Place a metal round rack in the bottom of a large stock pot. I recommend using at least a 12 quart pot, 12-15" in diameter for this recipe and cooking method. You can also use a full 12" deep stainless steel hotel pan with a rack in the bottom. The rack holds the food off the bottom and helps prevent it from burning or sticking and helps the steam to form.

If using the seaweed, place the seaweed on the bottom of the pan. Add the potatoes, place the corn, standing up around the outer edge of the pot or pan. Sprinkle with pepper and the fresh thyme sprigs. Add the lobster. Wrap the mussels and clams loosely in some cheesecloth and place them on top of the lobsters. Pour the white wine broth over the top, cover the whole pot with more seaweed or use the corn husk. cover with a lid or tightly with foil.

Place the pot on the fire and cook until a strong stream of steam is forming. Reduce the heat to medium and cook for at least 15 minutes. Until lobsters are red and cooked.

Approximate Cooking Time: 45 minutes

Special Note:
Serve with lots of melted butter.

Spiced Shrimp & Scallop Kabobs

4 portions

Ingredients:

1 pound	*Fresh Scallops*
1 pound	*16/20 ct. Shrimp. peeled and clean, tails on*
4 TB.	*Blackened Seasoning (p. 115)*
1/4 cup	*Melted Butter*

Heat Source:
Direct fire, medium heat then low heat (reference pg. 7-10)

Preparation:
Clean the shrimp and drain the scallops. Place the shrimp and scallops on a plate and season each side with the blackened seasoning. The amount of hotness will depend on how much seasoning is used. I prefer them pretty well seasoned. Skewer the shrimp and scallops on a 8" bamboo skewer, either together or as separate kabobs.

Preheat the grill, using medium high heat. Lightly oil the grates. Place the kabob on the grill and grill on each side for 3-4 minutes. After you turn them the first time, lightly brush them with the melted butter, to keep them from drying out.

Approximate Cooking Time: 6-8 minutes

Special Note:
Try the Gazpacho Salsa (pg. 187) with this one!

BBQ Grilled Salmon

4 portions

Ingredients:

2 pounds	*Fresh Salmon, skinless, cut in 8 oz. portions*
1/2 cup	*Backyard BBQ Mop (p.167)*

Heat Source:
Direct fire, medium heat (reference pg. 7-10)

Preparation:
Prepare the BBQ Mop and hold warm for grilling. Prepare the salmon fillets, remove the bones from the fillet.

Preheat the grill, using medium high heat. Lightly oil the grill. Lay the salmon fillets on the grill skin side up. Brush the skin side of the salmon with the mop before you turn it. Cook the salmon for about 4 minutes per side. Once you turn the salmon, brush it with the BBQ Mop and continue grilling until done. Brush or mop the fillet of salmon several times as it is grilling

Approximate Cooking Time: 8-10 minutes

Special Note:
Serve up with fresh lemon wedges.

Grilled Garlic Crablegs

4 portions

Ingredients:

2-3 pounds	*Crablegs, thawed, split*
1/2 cup	*Fresh Garlic Butter*

Heat Source:
Direct fire, medium heat (reference pg. 7-10)

Preparation:
Place the crablegs on a cutting board and split the legs in half, exposing the crabmeat.

Preheat the grill, using medium heat. Lightly oil the grill. Lay the crablegs on the grill with the split side down (meat expose to the grill). Grill the legs for about 2 minutes. The meat in crablegs are already cooked. Turn the legs over with the shell side down and top the expose meat with the softened garlic butter. Close the lid of the grill and cook the legs until hot and butter is melted into the meat and shell. Remove the crablegs and serve immediately with lots of fresh lemon wedges.

Approximate Cooking Time: 6 minutes

Fresh Garlic Butter (1/2 cup)

1/2 cup	*Sweet Butter, unsalted, soft*
1 each	*Juice of Lemon*
2 TB.	*Garlic, fresh, peeled, minced finely*
1 TB.	*Italian Parsley, fresh, minced*

Combine the softened butter with the remaining ingredients and mix well. Hold butter soft, not melted, for topping the crablegs.

Simple Seafood

Worth Raving About Rotisserie Meats

Lemon Pepper Thyme Whole Chicken

2-4 portions
Ingredients:

2 1/2 pound	Whole Chicken, washed and tied
1/2 cup	Lemon Pepper Seasoning
2 TB.	Fresh Thyme Leaves, minced
1/2 cup	Melted Butter. warm
2 each	Juice of Lemons

Heat Source:
Medium heat (reference pg. 10 & 47)

Preparation:
Wash the chickens in a solution of cold water and lemon juice. Rinse well and pat dry. Mix the lemon pepper and fresh thyme leaves together and rub the chicken on all sides with the rub.

Tie the legs together and tuck the wings underneath the back bone of the chicken. You may want to truss the chickens with butchers twine to help hold its shape as it turns. Place the rubbed chicken in the refrigerator to air dry for at least 24 hours.

Preheat the rotisserie. While the rotisserie is heating, place the chicken on a spit and center it before fastening with the prong holders. Place the spit on the rotisserie of your grill and turn on the motor. Check to make sure that the chicken is balanced on the spit, if not, a counter weight can be used on the end of the spit rod.

Allow the chicken to cook, for at least 30 minutes, after the skin is starting to get crisp, start to baste the chicken with the lemon butter. Baste the chicken every 15 minutes until the chicken is done. Chicken is done when internal temperature reaches 165° F.

Approximate Cooking Time: 45-60 minutes

Special Note:
The squeezed lemons can be placed inside the chickens before placing on the spit. Rotisserie cooking is a great time to apply a smoke flavor to your product, because of the longer cooking time.
I recommend using apple wood with this recipe.

Holiday Turkey
12 to 14 pound Turkey

Ingredients:

1 each	*12-14# Whole Turkey, fresh*
6 cups	*Water*
3 cups	*Maple Syrup, real*
2 TB.	*Molasses*
2 TB.	*Lime Juice, fresh*
2 TB.	*Kosher Salt*
2 TB.	*Onion Juice*
4 each	*Bay Leaves*
20 each	*Peppercorns, whole*
4 each	*Garlic Cloves, minced*
2 teaspoon	*Ginger, ground*
4 teaspoons	*Mustard Seed, whole*

Heat Source:
Low heat (reference pg. 10 & 47)

Preparation:
Combine all the ingredients together except the turkey and bring to a boil for 3 minutes. Remove from the heat and let cool down in a glass bowl. Reserve some of the brine for use in keeping the turkey moist as it cooks. Brine the turkey for 24 hours, turning to ensure that the whole turkey gets brine on it. When ready to rotisserie, remove from the marinade and pat dry with a paper towel before placing on to the spit rod.

Run the rod through the turkey, using the spit prongs to hold the turkey in place. You may want to truss the turkey with butchers twine to help hold its shape as it turns. Place the spit on the rotisserie of your grill and turn on the motor.. Check to make sure that the turkey is balanced on the spit, if not, a counter weight can be used on the end of the spit rod. Cook turkey until internal temperature is 165° F.

Approximate Cooking Time: 2 1/2 - 3 hours

Special Note:
Rotisserie cooking is a great time to apply a smoke flavor to your product, because of the longer cooking time. I recommend using maple wood with this recipe.

Red Hens
3 - 4 portions

Ingredients:

3 each	Cornish Game Hens
2 cups	Cranberry Juice
1/2 cup	Olive Oil
4 TB.	Chili Powder
1/2 cup	Honey
2 teaspoons	Onion Juice
1/3 cup	Balsamic Vinegar
2 TB.	Dry Mustard
2 TB.	Paprika
1 teaspoon	Basil
1/2 teaspoon	Red Pepper, ground
1/3 cup	Soy Sauce
1/4 cup	Hoisin sauce
1 TB.	Celery Salt

Heat Source:
Medium heat (reference pg. 10 & 47)

Preparation:
Combine all ingredients together, except the hens, and mix well. Thoroughly rinse and dry the hens, inside and out. Place the hens in a large container and cover with the brine, make sure they are completely submerged. If pot is not big enough to submerge them, you will need to turn them every 8 hours. Brine the hens for 24 hours under refrigeration. Remove the hens from the brine rinse off lightly and pat dry.

Run the spit through the hens, using the spit prongs to hold the hens in place. You may want to truss the hens with butchers twine to help hold their shape as they turns. Place the spit on the rotisserie of your grill and turn on the motor. Check to make sure that the hens are balanced on the spit, if not a counter weight can be used on the end of the spit rod. Cook hens until internal temperature is 165° F.

Approximate Cooking Time: 30-45 minutes

Special Note:
Rotisserie cooking is a great time to apply a smoke flavor to your product, because of the longer cooking time. I recommend using cherry wood with this recipe.

Rotisserie Meats

Mustard & Herb Crusted Prime Rib

10-12 people

Ingredients:

1 each	*5-6# Prime Rib, boneless*
1 1/2 cups	*Stone Ground Mustard*
1 cup	*Rotisserie Prime Rib Seasoning (p. 172)*

Heat Source:
Medium heat (reference pg. 10 & 47)

Preparation:
Allow the Prime rib to sit for 30 minutes at room temperature to remove the chill from the meat. Coat the entire Prime Rib with the stone ground mustard. Evenly coat the Prime Rib with the seasoning blend, covering all sides of the Prime Rib.

Using a spit, pierce the center of the Prime Rib, use spit prongs to hold the Rib in place and place on the rotisserie turn the motor on. Check to make sure that the prime rib is balanced on the spit, if not, a counter weight can be used on the end of the spit rod. Cook the Prime Rib until medium rare, remove when the internal temperature reaches 125° F. Allow the meat to rest for 30 minutes, before carving.

Approximate Cooking Time: 45-60 minutes

Special Note:
Rotisserie cooking is a great time to apply a smoke flavor to your product, because of the longer cooking time. I recommend using mulberry or sassafras wood with this recipe.

BBQ Mopped Whole Turkey

6-8 portions

Ingredients:

1 each	*10-12# Turkey Breast, bone-in*
3 TB.	*Lemon Pepper*
1 batch	*Backyard BBQ Mop, warmed (p. 167)*

Heat Source:
Medium heat (reference pg. 10 & 47)

Preparation:
Buy the Turkey Breast on the bone, to ensure a fresher product and better meat. De-bone the breast meat from the breast bone on both sides. Giving you two half breast. Season the breast meat with the lemon pepper on all sides.

Lay the breast, one on top of the other, with small ends against the larger end, to form a even thickness from end to end. Tie the breast together with butcher twine, looping about 5 times all the way across the breast at 1" intervals. This will help the breast meat to cook evenly and hold its shape on the spit. Marinate the tied breast meat in the mop for 4 hours before cooking

Slide the spit rod through the center of the tied breast meat, being careful not to pierce the meat itself. Use spit prongs to hold the turkey in place. Place the spit on the rotisserie of your grill and turn on the motor. Check to make sure that the turkey is balanced on the spit, if not, a counter weight can be use on the end of the spit rod. Cook until internal temperature is 165° F.

Approximate Cooking Time: 1 1/2 -2 hours

Special Note:
Rotisserie cooking is a great time to apply a smoke flavor to your product, because of the longer cooking time. I recommend using white oak wood with this recipe.

Marinated Pork Loin

6-8 portions

Ingredients:
2 each	*2# Pork Loins, boneless*
1 recipe	*All Purpose Marinade (p. 95)*

Heat Source:
Medium heat (reference pg. 10 & 47)

Preparation:
Trim the pork loins of any excessive fat. Lay the pork loins one on top of the other, with small ends against the larger end, to form an even thickness from end to end. Tie with together butcher twine, looping about 6 times all the way across the loin at 1" intervals. This will help the meat to cook evenly and hold its shape on the spit. Marinate the tied Pork loin in the marinade for 4 hours before cooking.

Slide the spit rod through the center of the tied pork loin, being careful not to pierce the meat itself. Use spit prongs to hold the pork loin in place. Place the spit on the rotisserie of your grill and turn on the motor. Check to make sure that the pork loin is balanced on the spit, if not, a counter weight can be used on the end of the spit rod. Cook until internal temperature is 155° F.

Approximate Cooking Time: 45 minutes

Special Note:
Rotisserie cooking is a great time to apply a smoke flavor to your product, because of the longer cooking time. I recommend using fruit wood with this recipe.

Crispy Rubbed Duck

2 people

Ingredients:

1 each	*4 -5 # Duckling*
2 TB.	*Garlic, fresh, minced*
2 TB.	*Kosher Salt*
1 TB.	*Rosemary Leaves, fresh, minced*
1 tsp.	*Paprika*
1 tsp.	*Poultry Seasoning*
1 tsp.	*Thyme Leaves, dried*
1 tsp.	*Oregano Leaves, dried*
1 tsp.	*White Pepper, ground*

Heat Source:
Medium heat (reference pg. 10 & 47)

Preparation:
Remove the innards from the duck and wash with cold water, drain and pat dry. Prepare the dry rub and mix well. Rub the seasonings well inside and out on the duck. Truss the duck legs to hold them together.

Slide the spit rod through the duck, use spit prongs to hold the duck in place. Place the spit rod on the rotisserie of your grill and turn on the motor. Check to make sure that the duck is balanced on the spit, if not, a counter weight can be used on the end of the spit rod. Cook until internal temperature is 165° F.

Approximate Cooking Time: 1 hour

Special Note:
Rotisserie cooking is a great time to apply a smoke flavor to your product, because of the longer cooking time. I recommend using fruit wood with this recipe.

Minted Leg of Lamb
8-10 people

Ingredients:

1 each	*5-6# Leg of Lamb, boneless & tied*
1 batch	*Lamb Marinade (p. 92), cold*
1 bulb	*Garlic Cloves, whole, peeled*

Heat Source:
Medium heat (reference pg. 10 & 47)

Preparation:
Cut small slits in the leg of lamb and in each slit push a whole clove of garlic into it. Stud the leg with at least 10 cloves of garlic. Place the lamb in a deep pan and pour the marinade over the whole lamb leg. Marinate lamb for at least 12 hours, but no more than 24 hours. Turning if needed. Once the lamb has marinated, remove from the marinade and drain well. Reserved the drained marinade for basting.

Run a rotisserie spit through the center of the leg, using spit forks to hold the lamb on each side. Place on the rotisserie motor on your grill and turn on. Check to make sure that the lamb is balanced on the spit, if not, a counter weight can be used on the end of the spit rod.

Baste every 30 minutes until done.

Cook until medium rare, remove when internal temperature is 125° F. Let rest for 20 minutes before slicing.

Approximate Cooking Time: 45-50 minutes

Special Note:
Rotisserie cooking is a great time to apply a smoke flavor to your product, because of the longer cooking time. I recommend using pecan wood with this recipe. Dry Rosemary branches also will add a nice flavor to this item, added seperately or in combination with wood.

Finger Sticky Chicken Legs

6-8 people

Ingredients:

20 each	Chicken Legs, as needed
2 TB.	Salt & Pepper, 50/50 mix
12 ounces	Honey
8 ounces	Liquid Margarine
1 cup	Hot Sauce
3/4 cup	Hoisin sauce
1/3 cup	Barbecue Sauce, your favorite
3 TB.	Asian Chili Garlic Paste
2 TB.	Molasses

Heat Source:
Medium heat (reference pg. 10 & 47)

Preparation:
Place all the ingredients except chicken, salt and pepper into a mixing bowl, using a whip blend the ingredients together very well. Completely blend the ingredients until a uniform color is achieved.

Season the chicken legs with the salt and pepper and then allow to air dry for about 1 hour.

You will need to use a Rotisserie Basket for this item. Slide the basket on to the spit rod, before filling. Fill the basket with the seasoned chicken legs and place the rod and basket on the grill with the rotisserie motor. Turn the motor on.

After about 15 minutes, begin to mop the chicken legs with the liquid mixture, mop the legs every 15 minutes until the mop is gone.

Cook until internal temperature of 165° F

Approximate Cooking Time: 30-45 minutes

Special Note:
Rotisserie cooking is a great time to apply a smoke flavor to your product, because of the longer cooking time. I recommend using sassafras wood with this recipe. Be careful with this mop, since it has a lot of BBQ sauce and honey, it may start to burn. If this starts to happen turn the heat down to low, or use indirect fire.

Award Winning BBQ Sauces & Dry Rubs

Rib Stars™ Double "J" BBQ Sauce

2 quarts

Ingredients:

5 cups	Ketchup
1/2 cup	Brown Sugar, golden brown
1/2 cup	Corn Syrup, Light
1/2 cup	Honey
1/4 cup	Molasses
1/2 cup	Yellow Mustard, pourable
1/3 cup	White Vinegar
3 TB.	Lemon Juice, fresh
1/3 cup	Onion Juice
1/4 cup	Worcestershire sauce
2 TB.	Rub Me Tender BBQ Rub (p. 168)
2 TB.	Celery Seed
2 TB.	Maggi ® Seasoning
2 tsp.	Liquid Smoke flavoring
1/2 TB.	Kitchen Bouquet®
1 tsp.	Black Pepper, table grind

Preparation:

Combine all ingredients together and blend well. Bring to a full boil, reduce and simmer for 1 hour, until slightly thickened. Remove from the heat and hold for service or cool completely and store in refrigerator until needed.

Special Note:

This sauce is on the sweeter side of BBQ sauces. Maggi® Seasoning can be found in most stores by the steak sauce and liquid smoke aisles.

Rib Stars™ Hawg's Breath BBQ Sauce

2 quarts

Ingredients:

1 quart	Ketchup
1/3 cup	Horseradish, hot, prepared
2/3 cups	Chicken Broth, canned
2/3 cups	White Vinegar
1/3 cup	Corn Syrup, light
2 tsp.	Dry Mustard
2/3 cups	Brown Sugar, golden brown
1 TB.	Shallot, minced
2/3 cups	Worcestershire sauce
2 TB.	Hot Sauce
1 TB.	Kosher salt
2 tsp.	Rib Stars™ Hawg's Breath BBQ Rub (p. 169)
1 TB.	Kitchen Bouquet®
2 ounces	Pick-a-pepper® Sauce
1 tsp.	Black Pepper, table grind

Preparation:

Mix the Worcestershire Sauce and dry mustard together to disolve the mustard completely, this helps to keep the dry mustard from forming clumps in the sauce. Combine all the rest of the ingredients together and add the mustard/worcestershire to the mixture, blend well. Bring to a boil and simmer for 1 hour to reduce slightly. DO NOT ALLOW THE SAUCE TO SCORCH!

Remove from the heat and hold for service or cool completely and store in the refrigerator until needed.

Teriyaki BBQ Sauce
5 cups

Ingredients:

1 1/2 cups	*Tomato Puree, canned*
3/4 cups	*Pineapple Juice, canned*
3/4 cups	*Soy Sauce, low sodium*
1 cups	*Rice Wine Vinegar*
1/2 tsp.	*Ginger, ground*
1/2 cups	*Molasses, unsulphured*
1 tsp.	*Caramel Color*
1/4 pound	*Brown Sugar, dark brown*
1 tsp.	*Garlic Powder*

Preparation:

Place all ingredients in a large sauce pot. Stir with a whip to blend ingredients thoroughly, then place on the stove and bring to a full boil. As soon as the sauce boils, allow to simmer ONE MINUTE ONLY, then cool the sauce and place in a container for storage and refrigerate until needed.

Special Note:

Great on chicken and grilled shrimp!

Cajun BBQ Sauce
1 quart

Ingredients:
1 1/2 TB.	Dry Mustard Coleman's®
1 ounces	Grain Mustard Stone ground
1 tsp.	Garlic Powder
1/2 teaspoon	Ginger, ground
1 1/2 tsp.	Chili powder
1 teaspoons	White Pepper
1 teaspoons	Red Pepper, crushed
1 ounces	Worcestershire sauce

Preparation:
Combine all the dry ingredients, mustard and Worcestershire together in a sauce pot to from a smooth paste. This helps the spices from forming clumps in the sauce.

1/2 cup	Cider vinegar
1/2 cup	Orange Juice, concentrate
2 cups	Chili Sauce
1/2 cup	Molasses
1/2 cup	Chicken Broth, canned
1/2 cup	Corn Syrup, light
2 ounces	Soy Sauce, lite

Preparation:
Add the remaining ingredients and liquids to the paste and blend well. Place on the heat and bring to a boil. Reduce the heat and simmer until the sauce is thickened (able to coat the back of a ladle). Remove and store until needed.

Special Note:
Excellent on shrimp!
Great on chicken and pork tenderloin.

Backyard BBQ Mop for Basting

2 cups

Ingredients:

12 ounces	*Margarine, melted*
1/2 cup	*White Vinegar*
2 tsp.	*Worcestershire sauce*
2 tsp.	*A-1® Steak Sauce*
1 tsp.	*Hot Sauce*
1 TB.	*Lemon Pepper*
3/4 cup	*Barbecue Sauce, your favorite*

Preparation:

Melt the margarine, and remove from the heat. Add the remaining ingredients, stir to blend well. Hold warm for mopping product while cooking.

Special Note:

This Mop is created for the use in Rotisserie cooking of turkey and chicken breast meat.

Enough for 5 pounds of meat.

Rib Stars™ Rub Me Tender BBQ Rub

1 1/2 cups

Ingredients:

1/4 cup	*Kosher Salt*
1/4 cup	*Seasoning Salt*
1/2 cup	*Turbinado Sugar (sugar in the raw)*
2 TB.	*Paprika*
2 TB.	*Chili Powder*
2 TB.	*Black Pepper*
2 TB.	*Garlic Salt*
2 TB.	*Granulated Onion*
1 TB.	*Cayenne Pepper*
1 TB.	*Lemon Pepper*

Preparation:

Mix all ingredients together well. Sprinkle over the both sides of the meat to be grilled.

Special Note:

If HOTTER is desired, increase the amount of cayenne pepper!!

Turbinado Sugar can be found in most grocery store, it is often referred to as Sugar in the Raw.

Rib Stars™ Hawg's Breath BBQ Rub

1 1/4 cups

Ingredients:

1/2 cup	*Turbinado Sugar, (sugar in the raw)*
1/4 cup	*Kosher Salt*
2 TB.	*Chili Powder*
1 TB.	*Granulated Onion*
1 TB.	*Granulated Garlic*
1 TB.	*Paprika*
1 TB.	*Black Pepper, fine grind*
1 TB.	*White Pepper, fine grind*
1 TB.	*Cayenne Pepper, ground*
1 tsp.	*Cumin, ground*
1 tsp.	*Allspice, ground*
1 tsp.	*Oregano, ground*

Preparation:

Mix all ingredients together well. Sprinkle over the both sides of the meat to be grilled.

Special Note:

If HOTTER is desired, increase the amount of cayenne pepper!!

Turbinado Sugar can be found in most grocery store, it is often referred to as Sugar in the Raw.

Memphis Style Dry Rub

1 1/2 cups

Ingredients:

1/2 cup	*Turbinado Sugar (sugar in the raw)*
1 TB.	*Granulated garlic*
2 TB.	*Onion Powder*
1 1/2 TB.	*Chili Powder*
2 tsp.	*Lemon Pepper*
1 TB.	*Paprika*
1 TB.	*Kosher salt*
2 tsp.	*Seasoning Salt*
1 tsp.	*Basil Leaves, dry*

Preparation:

Combine all ingredients and blend well, store in an air tight container until needed

Special Note:

Sprinkle seasoning to both sides of the rib.
Best on Spare Ribs.

Turbinado Sugar can be found in most grocery store, it is often referred to as Sugar in the Raw.

Backyard Chicken BBQ Rub

1 1/2 cups

Ingredients:

1/2 cup	*Turbinado Sugar, (sugar in the raw)*
1/4 cup	*Onion Salt*
1/4 cup	*Garlic salt*
1/4 cup	*Paprika, sweet*
2 tsp.	*Lemon Pepper*
2 tsp.	*Chili Powder*
2 tsp.	*Poultry Seasoning*
2 tsp.	*Black Pepper, table grind*
1/2 tsp.	*Cumin, ground*
1/2 tsp.	*Cayenne, ground*

Preparation:
Mix all ingredients together well. Sprinkle over the marinated chicken pieces.

Special Note:
Sprinkle rub on chicken after marinating, if you are marinating your chicken. Never use a heavy amount of rub on chicken. A light coat of rub is all that is needed on chicken.

Turbinado Sugar can be found in most grocery store, it is often referred to as Sugar in the Raw.

Rotisserie Prime Rib Seasoning

1 1/2 cups

Ingredients:

1/2 cup	*Kosher Salt*
1/4 cup	*Rubbed Sage*
1/4 cup	*Thyme Leaves, dry*
1/4 cup	*Oregano Leaves, dry*
1/4 cup	*Coarse Ground Black Pepper*

Preparation:
Combine all ingredients and blend well, store in an airtight container until needed

Special Note:
Rub into all sides of the prime rib, before placing on the rotisserie.

Standout
Side Dishes

Balsamic Grilled Asparagus

4 to 6 people

Ingredients:

2 pounds	*Asparagus, fresh, lightly blanched*
1/2 cup	*Balsamic Vinegar*
1/4 cup	*Brown Sugar*
as needed	*Fresh Ground Black Pepper*

Heat Source:
Direct fire, medium heat (reference pg. 7-10)

Preparation:
Lightly blanch or steamed the fresh asparagus until al dente and cool completely. Once cooled, placed the cooked asparagus in a shallow dish. Mix the vinegar and brown sugar together. Pour over the asparagus and let sit at room temperature for 30 minutes.

Preheat the grill, drain the asparagus and save the vinegar. Place the vinegar/sugar mixture in a small pan and place on the grill. Allow the mixture to cook while the asparagus is cooking. Vinegar will thicken slightly. Grill the asparagus over the medium heat, turning often. Cook the asparagus until just heated, about 5 minutes. Place back in a shallow dish and pour the sugar vinegar back over the asparagus. Cover with saran wrap and hold until service, about 10 minutes. Then serve.

Approximate Cooking Time: 5 minutes

Special Note:
Asparagus can also be done on a griddle top, with the vinegar mixture poured over the asparagus. Allow both the asparagus and vinegar mixture to cooked together.

Marinated Squash Ribbons

4 to 6 people

Ingredients:

1 pound	*Zucchini, washed*
1 pound	*Yellow Squash, washed*
1/2 cup	*Olive Oil*
1 TB.	*Lemon Juice, fresh*
1 TB.	*Cracked Black Pepper*
1 TB.	*Thyme Leaves, fresh*

Heat Source:
Direct fire, medium heat (reference pg. 7-10)

Preparation:
After washing the squashes, cut the ends off and cut into 1/4" thick slices, running the full length of the squash. Place the ribbon slices on a sheet tray. Combine the oil, lemon juice, black pepper and thyme leaves together and pour over the ribbon slices. Turn to slices over to coat on both sides. Allow to marinate for 30 minutes.

Preheat the grill, once the grill is hot place the slices across the grates. Cook about 1 minute and rotate the slices 90° to achieve a crisscross pattern. Cook another minute and turn the squash over, repeating the crisscross grilling process again. Remove the ribbons from the heat and serve.

Approximate Cooking Time: 3-4 minutes

Grilled Veggie Kabobs

6 people

Ingredients:

2 each	Red Pepper, seeded cut into 1" square pieces
2 each	Green Pepper, seeded cut into 1" square pieces
2 each	Zucchini, 1/2" slices
2 each	Yellow Squash, 1/2" slices
6 each	Cherry Tomatoes, whole
6 each	Mushroom Caps. whole
6 each	Red Onion, 1" wedges
as needed	Olive Oil
as needed	Salt & Pepper
1/2 cup	Olive Oil
1/2 cup	Fresh Basil Butter, softened

Heat Source:
Direct fire, medium heat (reference pg. 7-10)

Preparation:
After preparing the vegetables. Place cut vegetables on a wooden skewer. Alternating pieces on the skewer.

Preheat the grill, once the grill is hot place the skewers, dipped lightly in seasoned oil mixture, across the grates. Cook about 3 minute. Turn the kabobs over and cook another 3 minutes, basting with the softened basil butter. Cook the kabobs until tender, but not overcooked. Remove from the grill and place on a platter, top with the remaining butter and serve.

Approximate Cooking Time: 6 minutes

Fresh Basil Butter (1/2 cup)

1/2 cup	Sweet Butter, unsalted, soft
2 TB.	Fresh Basil , fine chopped
1 TB.	Fresh Parsley, minced
pinch	White Pepper

Combine the softened butter with the remaining ingredients and mix well. Hold softened butter for topping the kabobs, this allows the butter to melt by the warmth of the vegetables.

Simple Baked Beans

10-12 servings

Ingredients:

1 27 oz. can	"BUSH"® Beans "Country Style BBQ"
1 16 oz. can	Pinto Beans, canned, rinsed
1 16 oz. can	Great Northern Beans, canned rinsed
1/4 cup	Brown Sugar
1/2 pound	White Onions, finely chopped
6 ounces	Tomato Paste
1/3 cup	Brown Sugar
1/4 cup	Molasses
1 TB.	Dry Mustard
1/4 cup	White Vinegar
1/2 cup	Water
1 TB.	Rub Me Tender Dry Rub (p. 168)
1 1/2 TB.	Chili Powder
1 TB.	Liquid Smoke flavoring

Heat Source:
Direct fire, low heat (reference pg. 7-10)

Preparation:
Place all the ingredients into a heavy baking pan, stirring well to blend all the ingredients well. Top the beans with the additional brown sugar. Place the beans on grill and allow to cook on low heat until beans are bubbling and hot.

Approximate Cooking Time: 30-45 minutes

Special Note:
Beans only need to be heated well to bring the flavors together. Meat can be added the beans for extra flavor.

Marinated Mushroom Kabobs for Steaks

6 servings

Ingredients:

2 pounds	*Button Mushrooms, washed*
1 cup	*A-1 Steak Sauce®*
6 each	*Whole Scallions, washed, sliced into 1" pieces*

Heat Source:
Direct fire, low heat (reference pg. 7-10)

Preparation:
Wash the mushrooms caps. Clean the scallions, and slice into 1" pieces. Place the caps in a bowl and pour the steak sauce over them. Allow to marinate for one hour. Using wooden bamboo skewers, place the mushrooms and scallion pieces on the kabob in alternating fashion.

Preheat the grill, once the grill is hot, place the mushroom kabobs on the grill and cook for about 3 minutes on each side, basting with remaining steak sauce. Cook mushrooms until just starting to softened. Remove from the fire and serve on top of grilled steaks.

Approximate Cooking Time: 5-6 minutes

Slow Grill Roasted Garlic Bulbs

4 people

Ingredients:

2 each	*Large garlic bulbs, whole*
as needed	*Olive Oil*

Heat Source:
Indirect fire, medium heat (reference pg. 7-10)

Preparation:
Peel the outer skins of the garlic only, don't expose the individual garlic cloves. Cut the bulb on the bottom side just enough so that the bulb sits flat. Cut about 1/4" to 1/2" off the top of the garlic bulb to expose the top parts of garlic clove. Drizzle the top of the garlic bulbs with a little bit of olive oil each.

Preheat the grill, once grill is hot, place the oiled bulbs in the grill, away from the heat. Close the grill and roast the garlic until soft like butter. Remove and serve with warm French or Italian bread.

Approximate Cooking Time: 1 1/2 hours

Special Note:
Cooking garlic slow roasted takes some time, but the the final roasted soft garlic is well worth the wait. Garlic should be soft enough to spread like butter. This is great item to do when doing a rotisserie item, because of the longer cooking time.

Jambalaya

10-12 servings

Ingredients:

1 1/2 cups	Rice, uncooked
1 pounds	Smoked Sausage, sliced 1/4' thick
1/2 pound	Ham, medium dice
1 pounds	Chicken Breast, medium dice
2 ounces	White Onions, medium dice
2 ounces	Celery, medium dice
1/2 each	Green Bell Pepper, medium dice
3 each	Green Onion, sliced thin
2 TB.	Chicken Base
1 each	Tomato Puree, 10 ounce can
1 1/2 TB.	Season Salt
1 TB.	Sweet Basil, dry
1 TB.	Oregano, dry
1 each	Bay leaf
1 TB.	Thyme Leaves, dry
1 TB.	Garlic Salt
2 TB.	Sugar
1 TB.	Worcestershire sauce
1 teaspoons	Cayenne Pepper, ground
3 cups	Water, warmed

Heat Source:
Direct fire, low heat (reference pg. 7-10)

Preparation:
Place the rice in a 4" deep disposable half pan. Add to the rice and the meats, vegetables, base, seasonings, tomato puree and water. Stir the jambalaya mixture together well, to mix in all ingredients and spices.

Place on the grill over a low heat fire. Bring rice to a boil. Cover the rice, allow to swell and continue to cook, to make sure all meats are cooked.

Approximate Cooking Time: 30 minutes

Special Note:
Notes: If rice comes out a little dry, don't worry.
Just combine a can of tomato puree with warm water. (50/50). Stir mixture into the rice as needed!

Standout Side Dishes

You'll Relish These Salsas & Relishes for Grilled Foods

Mango & Mint Salsa

Enough for 8-10 people.

Ingredients:

4 each	Mangos, peeled
4 each	Juice of Limes
1 each	Small Red Bell Pepper, seeded and minced
1 each	Jalapeno Pepper, seeded and minced
2 TB.	Fresh Mint, minced

Preparation:

Peel the mangos. Medium dice (1/2" cubes) the mangos and place them in a bowl.

Clean and seed the peppers including the jalapenos. Chop the peppers add them all to the diced mangos. Add the fresh lime juice and fresh mint, mix gently. Let sit for 4 hours in the refrigerator, before using.

Special Note:

Best when made 4 hours ahead of time.
Great with Seared Ahi Tuna, Scallops or Shrimp.

Cucumber Salsa

Enough for 8-10 people.

Ingredients:

4 medium	Cucumber, peeled and seeded, diced
1 medium	Red Onion, small diced
1 medium	Green Pepper, small diced
1 bunch	Green Onions, minced
1 medium	Jalapeno, seeded and minced
6 each	Roma Tomatoes, seeded and chopped
1 bunch	Cilantro, minced
1/2 cup	White Vinegar
1/4 cup	Salad Oil
to taste	Salt and pepper

Preparation:

Peel and deseed the cucumber. Medium dice (1/2" cubes) the cucumbers and place them in a bowl.

Clean and seed all the peppers including the jalapenos. Chop the peppers and tomatoes, add them all to the diced cucumbers. Add the cilantro, mix gently. Combine the vinegar and oil, pour over the mixture. Season with salt and pepper. Let sit for 4 hours before using in the refrigerator.

Special Note:

Best when made 4 hours ahead of time.
Excellent with chicken dishes, particularily grilled chicken breast.

Gazpacho Salsa

Enough for 12-15 people.

Ingredients:

12 each	Cucumber, peeled and chopped
4 each	Tomatoes, peeled, seeded and chopped
1 each	Red Onion, small diced
1 each	Red Pepper, small diced
1 each	Yellow pepper, small diced
1 each	Green pepper, small diced
1 bunch	Cilantro, minced
1/2 cup	Champagne Wine Vinegar
1/2 cup	Olive Oil
to taste	Salt and pepper
1/8 cup	Garlic, minced

Preparation:

Clean and dice (1/4" dice) the peppers and green onions. Peel and seed the cucumbers and dice the same size as the peppers and onions. Add the cilantro, vinegar, oil, garlic and seasonings to the mixture and mix well.

Refrigerate until needed or ready to serve.

Special Note:

Best when made 4 hours in advance.
Save this one for Grilled Shrimp or Seafood dishes!

Melon Cilantro Salsa

Enough for 20 people.

Ingredients:

1 medium	Honey Dew Melon, peeled, seeded and chopped
2 medium	Cantaloupe, peeled and chopped
1 small	Red Pepper, small diced
1 small	Red Onion, small diced
1 bunch	Cilantro, minced
1/4 cup	Honey, 100% clover
1/8 cup	Rice Wine Vinegar
2 1/2 TB.	Vegetable Salt
1/4 cup	Salad Oil
3 TB.	Tabasco Sauce (Green Jalapeno)
1 teaspoon	Black Pepper, cracked

Preparation:

Dice all the melons into a medium dice (1/2" cubes), fine dice the red peppers and onion. Clean and mince the cilantro, place all the ingredients in a bowl and mix well the vinegar, oil and seasoning, toss well.

Special Note:

Make sure to use ripened melons for a full flavor.

Best to let melon sit out for a day before making relish. Great with chicken or pork items.

Papaya Pineapple Salsa

Enough for 20 people.

Ingredients:

1 each	Pineapple, peeled & diced
2 each	Papaya, peeled, seeded and diced
1 each	Red and Green Bell Peppers, seeded & small dice
1/2 cup	Salad Oil
1 TB.	Sesame Seed Oil
1/4 cup	Cider Vinegar
to taste	Salt and Pepper

Preparation:

Dice (1/2" cubes) and combine the pineapple, papayas & red pepper in a stainless steel bowl & toss. Add the remainder of the ingredients & toss.

Special Note:

Make sure the papaya is fully ripe, before making relish.

Great with Swordfish, Tuna or Mahi!

Salsas & Relishes

Grilled Pineapple Salsa

Enough for 12-15 people

Ingredients:

1 each	Pineapple, peeled, cored, quartered
1 each	Red Bell pepper, seeds removed, 1/4" diced
1 each	Green Bell pepper, seeds removed, 1/4" diced
1 each	Red Onion, chopped fine
1/4 cup	Salad Oil
3 TB.	Cilantro, minced
2 TB.	Lime Juice, fresh
2 TB.	Chives, minced
2 TB.	Parsley, minced
1 each	Serrano Pepper, minced

Preparation:

Preheat grill to medium heat. Place pineapple on grill. Grill until just beginning to brown, about 3 minutes per side. Coarse chop (1/2") the pineapple. Mix with the bell peppers, onion, oil, cilantro, lime juice, chives, parsley and chiles. Season with salt and pepper to taste. Cover and refrigerate salsa for 2 hours.

Special Note:

Great on Grilled fish!! (i.e.: Swordfish steaks, Halibut).

Red & Yellow Tomato Relish

Enough for 10 people

Ingredients:

1 pounds	Vine Ripe Red Tomatoes, 1/2" diced
1/2 pound	Yellow Tomatoes, 1/2" diced
2 medium	Red Onions, diced
2 cloves	Garlic, minced
1 1/4 cups	Balsamic Vinegar
1/2 teaspoon	Red Pepper Flakes
2 TB.	Basil, fresh, minced
to taste	Salt and pepper
1/4 cup	Olive Oil

Preparation:

Wash and prepare the red and yellow tomatoes. After dicing , place in a bowl. Combine the remaining ingredients and mix well to form the dressing. Pour the dressing over the tomatoes and chill for at least 12 hours.

Special Note:

Best when made 24 hours in advance. Allow the tomatoes to come to room temperature before serving.

Warm Jalapeno Corn Relish
Enough for 10-12 people

Ingredients:

2 pounds	Corn Kernels, frozen
3 each	Roma Tomato, 1/2" dice
1 cups	Red and Green Bell peppers, seeds remove, 1/2" dice
3 each	Jalapeno, thinly sliced rounds
1/2 pound	Onion, medium dice
2 TB.	Garlic, chopped
1 TB.	Black Pepper, ground
1 TB.	Kosher salt
1 TB.	Chili Powder
1 TB.	Butter, melted

Preparation:
In butter sauté onions and peppers in a pan on the grill, until onions are translucent. Add remaining ingredients, cook for fifteen minutes and cool. Salt and pepper to taste.

Special Note:
Hold warm for serving or cool down and reheat when needed.
Great with Blackened Items.

Sweet Endings
to the Story

Grilled Pineapple

3 servings

Ingredients:

1 each	Pineapple, fresh, cored and peeled
4 TB.	Butter, unsalted
2 TB.	Brown Sugar
1/4 tsp.	Cinnamon, ground

Heat Source:
Direct fire, low heat (reference pg. 7-10)

Preparation:
Peel and core the whole pineapple or buy already peeled and cored in a plastic container. Slice the pineapple into rings about 1/2" thick (6 slices). Place the pineapple rings in a plastic container or shallow pan. Melt the butter on the grill. Once melted, dissolve the brown sugar and cinnamon in the butter, stirring to dissolve the sugar fully. Allow mixture to cool. Pour the cooled mixture over the pineapple rings and allow to sit for 2-4 hours!

Spray the grill with a food release spray, preferably butter flavor. Preheat the grill, once hot, remove the pineapple rings and place them on the grill. Grill for 2-3 minutes per side until slightly caramelized. While the pineapple is grilling, place the leftover butter/sugar mixture in a small pan and allow to heat on the grill while the pineapple is cooking.

When the pineapple is done, remove from the heat and place on a platter, pour the warm butter mixture over the rings and serve.

Approximate Cooking Time: 4-6 minutes

Special Note:
Great with French Vanilla Bean Ice Cream!

Grilled Pound Cake with Raspberries

4-6 servings

Ingredients:

1/2 cup	Red Raspberry Jelly, seedless
2 cups	Red Raspberry, fresh or frozen
1 each	9" Pound Cake
as needed	Pound Sugar

Heat Source:
Direct fire, medium heat (reference pg. 7-10)

Preparation:
Heat the grill, place the jelly in a small pan and heat until fully melted. Place the berries in a glass bowl and stir in the jelly mixing well. Place in the refrigerator to chill. Hold chilled for later.

Slice the pound cake into 10-12 slices about 1/2 inch thick. Spray the grill with a food release spray, preferably butter flavor. Grill the slices of pound cake on each side for 2 minutes, allowing to grill and toast slightly. Place the grilled pound cake on a platter and top with the raspberry sauce. Dust the whole platter with powdered sugar and serve warm.

Approximate Cooking Time: 4 minutes

Special Note:
Can be made with other berry sauce, just match the berries with the same flavor jelly.

Grilled Mixed Fruit with Almond Cream

4-6 servings

Ingredients:

2 each	Peaches, firm but ripe
2 each	Pears, firm but ripe, Bosc
2 each	Apples, Granny Smith's
2 cups	Heavy Cream
1/2 cup	Brown Sugar
2 TB.	Marshmallow Fluff
1/2 cup	Creme de Almond Liqueur
4 TB.	Melted Butter, unsalted
2 TB.	Granulated Sugar

Heat Source:
Direct fire, medium heat (reference pg. 7-10)

Preparation:
For the fruit, peel and core each fruit. Cut the fruit in half. Place the cut fruit in a bowl and toss with the melted butter and sugar.

Pour the heavy cream into the bowl of the mixing machine. Using the whip attachment, whip the cream until the cream streaks (ripples) as the whip is moving. The cream should be half whipped. When the cream is half whipped, add the sugar, marshmallow fluff and liqueur. Continue whipping until almost firm.

Spray the grill with a food release spray, preferably butter flavor. Place the fruit cut side down on the grill. Grill, turning every 5 minutes, until lightly brown and soft, but not mushy.

Remove the fruit from the grill and place on a platter with the Almond Cream.

Approximate Cooking Time: 15 minutes

Special Note:
Other fruits to use, nectarines, mangos or pineapples

Mock Grilled Bananas Foster

3 servings

Ingredients:

3 each	*Bananas, ripe but firm, peeled*
1 TB.	*Butter, unsalted*
6 TB.	*Brown Sugar*
1/4 tsp.	*Cinnamon, ground*
3/4 cup	*Honey, 100% clover*
2 TB.	*Banana Liqueur*
2 TB.	*Dark Rum*

Heat Source:
Direct fire, low heat (reference pg. 7-10)

Preparation:
Peel and quarter the bananas, place in a bowl and gently toss with the melted butter and half of the brown sugar.

Place the remaining brown sugar, cinnamon, and honey in a medium pot and bring to a boil on the grill. Soon as the mixture boils, remove it from the grill. Using a long handle whip, add the banana liqueur and the dark rum! **Be very careful when doing this, since the hot liquid and cool liquid will foam up quickly. Use a pot double the volume of the total liquid! This method is needed to help release the alcohol from the sauce.**

Spray the grill with a food release spray, preferably butter flavor. Remove the bananas from the butter mixture and grill on both sides until just warmed, 2-3 minutes per side. Do not allow the bananas to get mushy. Remove the bananas from the grill and place in a shallow bowl. Pour the Sauce over the bananas and serve.

Approximate Cooking Time: 5-6 minutes

Special Note:
Great when poured over French Vanilla Bean Ice Cream!

Grilled Peaches with Sweetened Mascarpone

3 servings

Ingredients:

3 each	Peaches, fresh, seeded, and cut in half
3 TB.	Butter, unsalted
1/2 cup	Mascarpone Cheese
2 TB.	Brown Sugar
1/4 tsp.	Cinnamon, ground

Heat Source:
Direct fire, low heat (reference pg. 7-10)

Preparation:
Cut the peaches in half and remove the seed.

Spray the grill with a food release spray, preferably butter flavor. Preheat the grill, once hot, brush the peach halves with the melted butter. Grill, turning several times until tender but not mushy.

While peaches are grilling, stir the brown sugar and cinnamon into the cheese, and mix well.

Place the grilled peaches in a small serving platter, spoon some of the cheese mixture into the hollow centers of the peaches.

Approximate Cooking Time: 8-10 minutes

Special Note:
Can be garnished with fresh mint and chopped pistachios.

Grilled Pears with Creamed Gorgonzola & Spiced Walnuts

3 servings

Ingredients:

3 each	Pears, ripe but firm, peeled, cut in half, cored
3 TB.	Butter, unsalted
1/2 cup	Gorgonzola Cheese, crumbled
1/2 cup	Mascarpone Cheese
1/4 cup	Cream Cheese
2 TB.	Heavy Cream

Heat Source:
Direct fire, low heat (reference pg. 7-10)

Preparation:
Peel and cut the pears in half and core the center.

Spray the grill with a food release spray, preferably butter flavor. Preheat the grill, once hot, brush the pear halves with the melted butter. Grill, turning several times until tender but not mushy.

While pears are grilling, whip the three cheeses and heavy cream together to a smooth paste. Place the cheese mixture in a small pastry piping bag with a rose tip. Hold the filled pastry bag chilled until pears are done.

Place the grilled pears in a small serving platter, pipe some of the cheese mixture into the hollow centers of the pears. Top with Spiced Walnuts.

Approximate Cooking Time: 10-12 minutes

Special Note:
Great served with an excellent port!

Spiced Walnuts(1 cup)

1 cup	Walnut, halves or peices
1/4 cup	Butter, melted
2 tsp.	Blackened Seasoning (pg. 115)

Toss the walnuts with the melted butter and seasoning. Roast in the oven at 350° for about 15 minutes. Hold at room temperature for serving.

Index

A, B

Appetizers: 55-70
    Baba Ghanough, 58
    BBQ Chicken Quesadilla, 63
    Beef Satay, 60
    Bruschetta, pesto, 67
    Cheese & Salsa Quesadilla, 62
    Chicken Satay, 68
    Crabcakes, 61
    Crab Stuffed Mushrooms, 64
    Deviled Shrimp, 69
    Fajita Quesadillas, 57
    Grape & Brie Quesadilla, 59
    Gorgonzola Mushrooms, 65
    Steamed Mussels, 66
BBQ Sauces: 161-168
    Backyard BBQ Mop, 167
    Cajun BBQ Sauce, 166
    Rib Stars Double "J", 163
    Rib Stars Hawg's Breath, 164
    Teriyaki BBQ Sauce, 165

C

Chicken, Plump & Juicy: 123-132
    Brick Grilled, 132
    Chicken Fajitas, 125
    Chicken Scaloppini, 128
    Herb Grilled Chicken, 126
    Rub Me Tender Chicken, 127
    Margarita Chicken, 129
    Roasted Chicken Thighs, 130
    Shish Taouk, 131
Care & Cleaning, 49-53
Cooking:
    Direct, 6
    Direct, gas, 10
    Indirect, 6
    Indirect, gas, 9

D

Desserts: 193-200
    Bananas Foster, mock, 198
    Mixed Fruit, almond cream, 197
    Peaches, grilled, 199
    Pears, grilled, 200
    Pineapple, grilled, 195
    Pound Cake, raspberries, 196
Dry Rubs: 169-172
    Chicken BBQ Rub, 171
    Memphis Style Rub, 170
    Rotisserie Prime Rib Rub, 172
    Rib Stars Rub Me Tender, 168
    Rib Stars Hawg's Breath, 169
Dry Rub, basics of, 29-30

F

Fuel Basics, 5-10
Fire Basics, 5-10
Fire:
    Banked Coal, 7
    Center Mounded Coal, 7
    Dual Off Set, 9
    Lighting, 5
    Off set Coal, 8
Food Safety: 22-23
    Buying, 22
    Equipment, 23
    Handling, 22
    Internal Temperatures, 23
    Leftovers, 23
    Storage, 22
    Thawing, 22

G

Gas Grill, starting, 6
Grill basics, 1-4
Grilling, 40-45
Grilling Chart, 41-45
Grilling Methods, 40
Grill:
  Charcoal, 2
  Gas, 1
Grilling Tips: 33-38
  Baking, 33
  Flare Ups, 34
  Herbs & Vines, 33
  Infused Oils, 34
  Poultry, 34
  Smoking, 36
  Steaks, 37
  Seafood, 35
  Shellfish, 35
  Wood & Meat, combinations, 37
Grilling Tools: 11-15
  Aprons & hats, 15
  Baskets, 11
  Brush, 11
  Drip Pans, 12
  Forks, 12
  Gloves & Mitts, 12
  Griddles, 12
  Grids & Screens, 12
  Mats, 13
  Planks, 13
  Skewers, 13
  Smoker Box, 14
  Spatulas, 14
  Spray Bottles, 14
  Thermometers, 15
  Tongs, 15

H, I

Herbs: 27-28
  Angelica, 27
  Basil, 27
  Bay Leaf, 27
  Dill, 27
  Fennel, 27
  Lemon Balm, 27
  Marjoram, 27
  Mint, 27
  Oregano, 27
  Parsley, 28
  Rosemary, 28
  Saffron, 28
  Sage, 28
  Savory. 28
  Tarragon, 28
  Thyme, 28
Infused Oils: 101-107
  Sage & Garlic, 103
  Rosemary & pepper, 104
  Roasted Red Pepper, 105
  Sundried Tomato, 106
Internal Temperatures, 23

M

Marinades: 89-100
  All Purpose, 95
  Coconut Curry, 99
  Lamb, 92
  London Broil, 94
  Margarita for Chicken, 91
  Mustard, shrimp, 96
  Orange Soy Hoisin, 97
  Tuscan, 93
  Fajita, 98
Marinating, effects of, 31-32
Meat, buying: 16-21
  Chicken Breast, 16
  Chicken, whole, 16
  Duck, whole, 17
  Fish Fillets, 17

Fish Steaks, 17
Fish Loins, 17
Lobster Tails, 17
Pork Loins, 18
Pork Tenderloin, 18
Prime Rib, 18
Ribs:
    Baby Back, 18
    Spare, 19
    St. Louis Style, 19
Scallops, 19
Shrimp, 19
Tenderloin, whole, 20
Turkey, whole, 20
Turkey Breast, 20
Turkey Chops, 20
Meats: Grilled & Seared, 107- 122
    Beef fajitas, 114
    Blackened Filet, 115
    Hawg's Breath Pork Ribs, 112
    Kifta, 117
    Lamb Chops, 113
    London Broil, 118
    Orange Soy Pork Loin, 120
    Spiced Tenderloin, 116
    Steak Au Poivre, 110
    Teriyaki Ribeye, 121
    Tuscan Grilled Steaks, 109
    Veal Scaloppini, 119
    World's Best Burgers, 111

P

Pizza, cracker crust: 71-80
    BBQ Chicken, 73
    Chicken Pesto, 80
    Garlic & Three Cheese, 76
    Margherita, 78
    Nostra, 79
    Pepperoni & Vidalia, 75
    Pesto, 74
    Shrimp & Scallop, 77

Poultry, Plump & Juicy: 123-132
    Brick Grilled, 132
    Chicken Fajitas, 125
    Chicken Scaloppini, 128
    Herb Grilled Chicken, 126
    Rub Me Tender Chicken, 127
    Margarita Chicken, 129
    Roasted Chicken Thighs, 130
    Shish Taouk, 131

R

Rotisserie Cooking, 46-48
Rotisserie Meats: 149-159
    Chicken Legs, sticky, 159
    Chicken, lemon pepper, 151
    Duck, crispy rubbed, 157
    Lamb, leg, minted, 158
    Pork Loin, marinated, 156
    Prime Rib, herb crusted, 154
    Red Hens, 153
    Turkey, holiday, 152
    Turkey, whole, BBQ, 155

S

Salads: 81-88
    Asparagus, 87
    Grilled Caesar, 83
    Grilled Chicken, 84
    Grilled Shrimp Nicoise, 85
    Oranges & Fennel, 86
Salsa & Relishes: 183-192
    Cucumber Salsa, 186
    Gazpacho Salsa, 187
    Jalapeno corn Relish, 192
    Mango & Mint Salsa, 185
    Melon Cilantro Salsa, 188
    Papaya Pineapple Salsa, 189
    Pineapple Salsa, grilled, 190
    Tomato Relish, 191

Seafood, simple: 133-147
   Ahi Tuna, seared, 137
   Clambake, 144
   Crablegs, garlic, 147
   Fish Tacos, 135
   Lobster Tail, scampi style, 143
   Salmon, BBQ, 146
   Scallops, coconut, curried, 140
   Scrod, buttered crumb, 138
   Shrimp, mustard, grilled, 139
   Shrimp, pesto wrapped, 141
   Shrimp & Scallop Kabobs, 145
   Swordfish, peppered, 136
   Trout, lemon pepper, 142
Searing, 39-40
Side Dishes: 173-182
   Baked Beans, simple, 178
   Balsamic Asparagus, 175
   Garlic Bulbs, 180
   Jambalaya, 181
   Mushroom Kabobs, 179
   Squash Ribbons, 176
   Veggie Kabobs, 177
Smoke, wood & meat chart, 36
Spices: 24-26
   Allspice, 24
   Anise, 24
   Caper, 24
   Caraway Seed, 24
   Cardamon, 24
   Cayenne, 25
   Celery Seed, 25
   Chili Powder, 25
   Cinnamon, 25
   Clove, 25
   Coriander, 25
   Cumin Seed, 25
   Dill Seed, 25
   Ginger, 25
   Mace, 26
   Nutmeg, 26
   Paprika, 26
   Pepper, 26
   White Pepper, 26

   Poppy Seed, 26
   Sesame Seed, 26
   Mustard, 26
   Turmeric, 26

T

Temperature Zones:
   Coal, 7
   Gas. 10
Temperature Chart, hand, 10

W

Wood & Meat combinations, 37

# Backyard Grilling Notes